A Practical Guide to Acquisitions

ABOUT THE AUTHOR

Denzil Rankine is chief executive of AMR, Europe's leading specialist in commercial due diligence.

Denzil studied law at the University of Kent and then after two years with R K Carvill in reinsurance broking, he moved into consultancy. In 1983 he joined PBD, a small business development research consultancy specialising in helping British companies to enter the US market. Over the following four years he played a leading role in growing the business, and at the same time visited 49 states in the USA.

In 1987 Denzil was invited to join the Seer Group, a management consultancy which had broken away from Deloitte & Coopers. Denzil founded the strategic research consultancy division of Seer, which worked alongside the corporate finance group. A number of Denzil's clients were in the defence electronics industry; as the disastrous nature of Ferranti's acquisition of ISC unfolded Seer responded, becoming one of the first consultancies to offer a specialised commercial due diligence service. Denzil founded AMR in 1991.

ABOUT AMR

AMR is a strategic research consultancy based in London. It was founded in 1991 and is Europe's leading specialist in commercial due diligence. AMR has investigated over 250 transactions on behalf of British, American and continental European acquirers in 26 countries. The value of these transactions ranges from £1 million to £400 million. AMR has also investigated a number of multibillion dollar cross-border mergers.

AMR's consultants have an average of eight years' strategic research experience, gained after earlier careers in operational roles. All are fluent in at least one language other than English.

AMR's clients include one of the world's top five media groups, France's largest electronics group and one of Britain's largest distribution companies. AMR's clients are mostly capitalised at over £1 billion, but it also works with a wide range of other smaller public and private companies.

A Practical Guide to Acquisitions

How to Increase your Chances of Success

DENZIL RANKINE

AMR International Ltd, UK

JOHN WILEY & SONS

Chichester · New York · Weinheim · Brisbane · Singapore · Toronto

Copyright © 1998 by John Wiley & Sons Ltd,
Baffins Lane, Chichester,
West Sussex PO19 1UD, England

National   01243 779777
International (+44) 1243 779777
e-mail (for orders and customer service enquires):
cs-books@wiley.co.uk
Visit our Home Page on http://www.wiley.co.uk
or http://www.wiley.com

Reprinted August 1998

Other Wiley Editorial Offices

John Wiley & Sons, Inc., 605 Third Avenue,
New York, NY 10158-0012, USA

WILEY-VCH Verlag GmbH, Pappelallee 3,
D-69469 Weinheim, Germany

Jacaranda Wiley Ltd, 33 Park Road, Milton,
Queensland 4064, Australia

John Wiley & Sons (Asia) Pte Ltd, 2 Clementi Loop #02-01,
Jin Xing Distripark, Singapore 129809

John Wiley & Sons (Canada) Ltd, 22 Worcester Road,
Rexdale, Ontario M9W 1L1, Canada

Library of Congress Cataloging-in-Publication Data

Rankine, Denzil.
  A practical guide to acquisitions: how to increase your chances of
  success / Denzil Rankine.
     p.   cm.
  Includes bibliographical references and index.
  ISBN 0-471-97598-2 (pbk.)
  1. Consolidation and merger of corporations.   I. Title.
  HD2746.5.R365   1997
  658.1'6—dc21   97–9427
                                                              CIP

British Library Cataloguing in Publication Data

A catalogue record for this book is availabe from the British Library

ISBN 0-471-97598-2

Typeset in 11/13pt Palatino from the author's disks by Vision Typesetting, Manchester.
Printed and bound in Great Britain by Bookcraft Ltd, Midsomer Norton, Somerset.
This book is printed on acid-free paper responsibly manufactured from sustainable
forestation, for which at least two trees are planted for each one used for paper
production.

Contents

List of Figures

List of Case Studies

List of Checklists

Foreword

As the pace of technological change increases and its availability becomes more and more widespread, companies are increasingly forced to concentrate on the things they do best, or suffer the consequences of being overtaken by those who do.

Conglomerates have had their day and the current focus is decisively on so-called core competencies. Invariably, this entails as a first step subjecting all parts of the organisation to the usual benchmarking tests of peer group efficiency. But then the two strategic criteria of critical mass and selective excellence will determine whether the future of those activities lies in retention, upgrading or disposal.

Equally, as governments around the world battle with their budgets, the move to follow the UK lead of successful privatisation of state-owned entities becomes irresistible.

In most major industries, too, be they oil, utilities, automobiles, airlines or pharmaceuticals, companies large and small are divesting, merging and making acquisitions to achieve lower-cost critical mass and higher standards of customer satisfaction.

These significant changes in the business environment will create great opportunities for the competent and astute acquirer as governments and companies reshape their portfolios. Whether it be through the snapping up of large company discards, management buyouts, the acquisition of private companies, or reorganisation of large corporate portfolios, the skills required for the successful acquisition that will give lasting shareholder value will have much in common.

Denzil Rankine's book is a very readable and admirable exposition of the wide range of factors that today's acquirers should consider in this era of major commercial and industrial change and opportunity.

Step by step, Mr Rankine takes aspiring acquisitors through all the necessary stages which, if achieved, should make the journey for them and their shareholders well worthwhile.

Sir Peter Walters

Preface

This guide is designed as a practical tool to assist acquirers to obtain the best results from acquisition. It is based on the experience and research of professional advisers specialising in acquisition, who have worked on transactions in the UK, continental Europe, North America and the rest of the world.

Much has been written on the subject of acquisition, particularly in the areas of accountancy and law; this guide focuses mostly on the less well-documented areas of strategy, marketing and the human factor.

Case studies have been included to emphasise critical issues and to illustrate how, or how not, to go about making acquisitions. Checklists are provided for the most important steps in the acquisition process.

AMR has conducted Europe's most comprehensive study of why acquisitions succeed or fail. Developed in co-operation with ICME Paris, a strategy consultancy specialising in post-acquisition integration, the study reviewed over 350 European transactions three years after their completion. The study evaluated in detail the impact of pre-acquisition decisions and post-acquisition actions. The success of acquisitions is defined by whether or not the acquisition met all or most of the criteria set out before the transaction took place. Many of the statements in this guide are backed by this study, and a number of figures are reproduced from it.

I would like to thank Calum Chace for his assistance in writing this guide.

DR

1
Introduction

A consensus emerges on a number of points from experienced practitioners, the AMR/ICME survey and other academic material:

- Acquisition is a risky business: at least half of all acquisitions fail to meet expectations.
- The shareholders of the seller often obtain a better return from a transaction than the shareholders of the acquirer.
- Many companies pay too much for acquisitions. This is the single greatest reason for failure.
- So-called synergies are nearly always overestimated.
- Diversification often fails to deliver desired returns to shareholders.

These results are unsurprising. In the competitive market of the 1980s there were more companies seeking to buy than there were attractive targets available. The result was that bargains were hard to find and sellers tended to do better than buyers.

For example, with the benefit of hindsight it is clear that Evode overpaid for Chamberlain Phipps, and this led to it being subsequently taken over by Laporte. Similarly in the advertising sector, BDDP was burdened with a debt mountain of $160 million at the start of the US recession when it acquired Wells Rich Greene. Saatchi & Saatchi and WPP were crippled by earn-out clauses on which they could not deliver. (See Case Study 1.)

The early 1990s saw a reversal as some of the more astute buyers waited for those who overpaid to suffer. Many struggling unquoted businesses that offered themselves for sale in the early 1990s failed to find new owners as it was clear to buyers that the assets would soon be on offer from the receivers. The mid 1990s saw a return to a more balanced market, mostly due to a wide range of macroeconomic factors. These included the low inflation and low interest rate environment, increased globalisation and the impact of the European Union. Nonetheless, many of the lessons learnt in more difficult economic times remain valid.

AGREED, NOT HOSTILE

The focus of this guide is mostly on the agreed acquisition of private businesses or the subsidiaries of quoted companies.

Most acquirers avoid contested bids. They are highly risky, partly because the quantity and quality of information available to assess the business is inevitably limited. For example, when Rentokil finally took control of BET in 1996 after an acrimonious battle, its management was surprised to find that the head office staff numbered less than a hundred, one-fifth of the total the aggressor expected. Although thorough investigation of a target is possible (and recommended) before and during a hostile bid, access to the target is bound to be limited.

In hostile bids a financial investigation can be conducted only on published information that is far from perfect. Management accounts, which are normally made available during the negotiation of an agreed deal, are far more revealing. Legal and environmental risks are also much harder to assess in contested bids and there is no opportunity to use the protection of warranties and indemnities. Hostile bids are also the subject of strict takeover rules.

SCOPE

This guide is not intended to be comprehensive. Its focus is primarily on commercial issues. Legal and financial issues are important in delivering value to shareholders but they have been written about extensively elsewhere.

This guide has been written for senior managers and others

responsible for acquisitions. It offers practical advice in the context of what they are trying to do with the business – create wealth for their shareholders.

The guide presents the main issues that require consideration in the context of any acquisition. It contains checklists, suggested approaches, case studies and examples from our experience of working across a wide range of acquisition activities. We hope you will find it useful and welcome any suggestions or comments for inclusion in future editions.

2
Creating Value for Shareholders

This guide presents a framework for considering how each of the steps which form part of the acquisition process should be taken if companies are going to avoid the pitfalls so often reported in the financial press. Table 2.1 overleaf sets out the steps in the process, and identifies the information required at each stage to produce the desired result.

This guide deals with each of the issues noted in Table 2.1.

The next chapter addresses the key strategy issues:

- Does the combined business make sense?
- What is the potential gain to the acquirer's shareholders?

Table 2.1   *Framework for value delivery.*

Practical steps	Information needed	Outputs and decisions
1 Strategic planning	Internal strengths and weaknesses	Chosen business development route(s)
	Basic knowledge of markets	Rationale for acquisition
		Screening criteria
2 Identification and selection of acquisition targets	What opportunites are available	List of candidates
	Quality and fit with acquirer	Prioritisation
3 Making contact	Who to approach and how	Platform for negotiation
		Ball park price
4 Evaluation	Target's potential contribution to the acquirer	Broad understanding of the potential target
5 Due diligence	The target's accounts, contractual arrangements, and market situation	Avoidance of bad deals
		Identification of risks to be avoided
		Basis for valuation and integration planning
6 Financial valuation	The real and perceived value of the business to both parties	A realistic price
7 Deal structuring	Financial and tax position of both parties	A framework to suit both sides
	Aspirations of the seller	
8 Detailed negotiation	Aspirations of the seller	A deal that delivers benefit to both sides
	The buyer's walk-away price	
9 Implementation planning	The target business' characteristics and structure compared with the acquirer's	Realisation of the potential gain to the acquirer's shareholders

3
Does Acquisition Make Sense?

ORGANIC GROWTH

Acquisition is not the only route to growth. Organic growth can be an excellent and significantly less risky alternative. For example, investors in GM found that organic growth through the GM credit card launch provided a return on investment far greater than any acquisitions might have brought. Likewise, Richard Branson has created major music, retail and airline businesses from scratch.

Particularly in the case of small acquisitions, would-be acquirers should review the alternatives offered by start-up. Other alternatives such as licence or joint venture may also be worth evaluating. In many cases the same financial evaluation methods can be used to assess competing development routes.

Nonetheless, acquisitions are a fact of business life, and they can be a powerful and efficient way to grow or improve a business' performance. They can sometimes provide significant improvement to shareholder value.

CORE COMPETENCES

All sorts of business combinations can make sense. However, Figure 3.1 (from the AMR/ICME survey) demonstrates how risk increases in cases where the acquirer buys a business outside known countries or existing product areas.

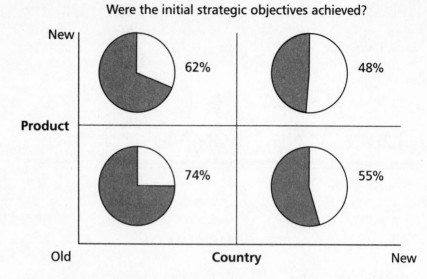

Figure 3.1   *"Stick to your knitting"* (*Source:* AMR/ICME survey).

Conventional wisdom promotes the philosophy of "sticking to your knitting". In the case of retailers such as Marks & Spencer and Sainsbury, a total concentration on retailing has generated strong brands and excellent organic growth, despite recent difficulties. But their retailing activities are extended to an increasingly wide range of consumer products: DIY for Sainsbury, and food, furniture and financial services for M&S. Identifying your core competences is not necessarily a simple matter.

"Sticking to your knitting" is the highly effective thinking practised by many successful groups. Senior managers are well advised to define their core competences carefully, probably (but not necessarily) in terms of products, geographic coverage, distribution clout or management skills. They should then ensure that any major investment falls within the scope of these competences.

Toys 'R' Us and the Early Learning Centre branched out from toys into children's clothing on the grounds that their purchasing power, brand name, retail outlets and sophisticated information systems would give them an edge. Similar logic persuaded Honda to diversify from motorcycles to lawnmowers and small cars; and Black & Decker from power tools to home appliances. These businesses worked out what they are strong at; they defined their core competences and then applied them to other businesses. This approach is as valid for acquisitions as for organic growth.

Not all major retailers possess the same set of core competences, and other factors can ruin an apparently logical business development move, as W. H. Smith and Boots discovered with their very expensive foray into the DIY business during a major downturn in the UK housing market. Adverse economic developments are hard to predict and even harder to compensate for.

Case Study 1 contrasts the various approaches to business development and acquisition that were adopted by advertising agencies and media buyers in France. In France, as in the UK, the industry went through many interesting stages of development and saw considerable growth and acquisition activity in the late 1980s and early 1990s. As with the French supermarket industry, wholesalers consolidated into powerful *Centrales* to obtain better prices from their suppliers.

Case Study 1 also demonstrates the pitfalls of unclear strategic thinking in the acquisition planning process.

CASE STUDY 1: CONCENTRATION IN FRENCH MEDIA BUYING

Background

While WPP and Saatchi & Saatchi attempted to build global multi-disciplinary marketing services groups, French media buying giants such as Carat focused on their core business and core competence of media buying. They used organic growth and acquisitions to such good effect that the attention of the Conseil de la Concurrence (France's equivalent of Britain's Monopolies and Mergers Commission) was attracted.

Developing Role of the *Centrales*

Until the early 1970s, advertising agencies were relatively small companies providing clients with a full service package in advertising, including research, strategic planning, the creation of advertising, media planning and the purchase of media space.

Centrales started to appear during the early 1970s as media brokers, purchasing large blocks of space for resale to clients at discounted rates. They then began providing media analysis and planning, formerly the exclusive domain of advertising agencies.

In the 1980s, while advertising agencies expanded their services beyond advertising, adding consultancy and even financial services, the *Centrales* concentrated on just one business. In 1980, 10% of advertising space was bought through *Centrales*; by 1992 the figure was 80%. The *Centrales'* scale advantages gave them substantial purchasing power. Both their suppliers (the media) and their customers (advertisers) benefited as the market grew. At the same time the *Centrales* were able to improve their margins by exploiting the media discount structures.

By 1993 French media buying had become a virtual oligopoly with four *Centrales* (Groupe Carat, TMP, PMS and Euro RSCG) sharing over 65% of the market. The diversified advertising agencies had been left behind and found themselves losing out.

Reactions

As the power of the *Centrales* grew, advertising agencies faced the threat of becoming little more than creative boutiques, losing their media planning and space buying roles. The agencies' plight was exacerbated by financial weakness brought on by high levels of gearing. Their plans to build large multi-service groups were proving to be strategically unsound as clients preferred high-quality, specialised services.

Several European advertising agencies reacted by forming joint ventures, such as TMP, to gain bargaining power with the media and thus regain market share.

The remaining small independent media buyers were forced to flee to contracting niches. Strategically they were faced with the awkward choice between forming alliances with the *Centrales* to gain negotiating power, or being acquired.

The Conseil de la Concurrence saved many of them from the horns of this dilemma by conducting an investigation and proceeding to liberalise the market by enforcing open media negotiations.

The ensuing transparency of pricing showed the media and advertisers how craftily the *Centrales* had been operating. The Centrales were then forced to introduce market-based discount structure, which greatly reduced their operating margins.

Conclusion

The advertising agencies followed the ill-fated acquisition-driven strategy of creating multidiscipline businesses which failed to deliver value to shareholders; meanwhile the *Centrales* focused on their core competences to such powerful effect that they had to be regulated.

CROSS-BORDER COMPLICATIONS

A number of factors can confound the philosophy of sticking to your knitting. These include the complications of cross-border management. M&S has been less than wholly successful in replicating its UK successes internationally. Only after a painful learning curve did France and Spain become successful markets for it; nearly ten years passed until the US acquisition Brooks Brothers could be described as successful.

Figure 3.1 shows that only 55% of the acquirers in our survey achieved their strategic objectives when they moved into a new country. Even fewer achieved their financial objectives. Case Study 2 at the end of this chapter profiles an initially expensive but successful cross-border acquisition strategy.

CULTURAL BARRIERS

Cultural incompatibilities can also be a hurdle: the Leeds Permanent and National & Provincial Building Societies found that the cultures of the two businesses were too far apart to merge. Happily, they pulled out before it was too late. Fisons, the British pharmaceutical company, suffered badly from unforeseen cultural conflict after acquiring VG Instruments.

INSTITUTIONAL BACKING FOR ACQUISITIONS

Although it is generally true that focusing on core competences is a good policy, the link between an acquirer's competences and their intended application can sometimes be obscure. Institutional investors have backed contested bids from buyers with no track record in the industry of their targets. Examples in the early 1990s included the bids by TI for Dowty, and Tomkins for RHM. This support is apparently based on the view that the bidders have strong management skills that will enable them to restructure and improve the businesses acquired. It does not always work: Tomkins found itself to be undervalued by the market for years after the RHM deal. Midlands Electricity found that it did not have the appropriate management skills to run burglar alarm businesses and had to reverse out at some considerable cost. The water utilities have also been disappointed by revenues from non-regulated activities, as set out in Table 3.1.

Hanson's demerger is based on the logic that shareholders had actually been investing in four unrelated businesses. The demerger was then designed to avoid bids and to improve the value of the overall business. Case Study 2 sets out the details.

Table 3.1   *Impact of non-core businesses water utilities.*

Company	Group turnover	Non-regulated turnover	Group operating profit*	Non-regulated profit*
Anglian	775.7	116.2	293.7	(5.2)
United Utilities	1838.6	259.4	488.6	18.8
Severn Trent	1157.5	261.9	422.7	27.9
Southern	424.7	61.2	170.6	11.2
South West	321.3	75.1	139.9	9.3
Thames	1193.6	218.0	365.7	(21.6)
Hyder	651.6	129.2	183.6	3.3
Wessex**	239.1	–	129.8	12.2
Yorkshire	579.6	58.1	220.4	7.7
Total	7181.7	1179.1	2414.0	63.6

Notes:
*Excluding exceptional items
**Wessex – UK Waste is treated as an associate
Sources: Company results for the year 1995–1996; Deutsche Morgan Grenfell

CASE STUDY 2: HANSON ACQUISITION AND DEMERGER: CREATING AND THEN REDUCING SHAREHOLDER VALUE

Creating Shareholder Value by Undoing Acquisitions

In the 1980s, Hanson was seen as one of the UK's most successful companies; it embodied the corporate style of that period. Its name rarely appeared in print without the word "acquisitive"; its highly successful takeover strategy made the company a conglomerate with a stock market value of £11 billion.

Hanson's raison d'être was the purchase of underperforming companies, the sale of peripheral assets, and a fierce focus on the profitability of what remained. This Hanson formula produced exceptional returns for shareholders. The classic example was Imperial Group, where some £2.4 billion of the original £2.5 billion purchase price was recouped from asset disposals, leaving Hanson with an intact tobacco business that was still generating £350 million in operating profits.

A comparable formula was worked in the USA, where Hanson was able to recover from disposals most of the price it paid for SCM in the USA, and still retain a profitable speciality chemicals company. (See Figure 3.2.)

Reducing Shareholder Value through Demerger

In the mid 1990s, Hanson had to cope with a set of unfamiliar problems. First, it had grown too large – and arguably too complex – for the kinds of acquisition that had fuelled its growth. Hanson's management found it increasingly difficult to find suitable acquisitions capable of making a big impact on earnings. Without big acquisitions, Hanson's weak cash flow was hard pressed to sustain its high dividend policy. Concerns over the appointment of successors to the founding Lord Hanson and White helped provoke an air of uncertainty.

In January 1996, Lord Hanson announced plans to demerge the company's principal businesses into four separate publicly quoted companies by the end of the year. The companies are: Energy,

Hanson Trust and SCM

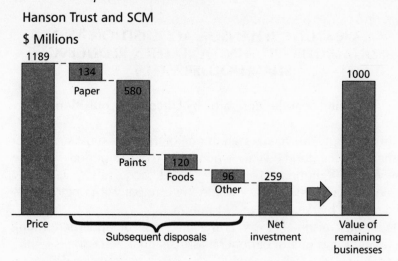

Figure 3.2   *Adding value by undoing acquisitions.*

Imperial Tobacco, Millennium Chemicals and Hanson (Building Materials & Equipment). Investors received shares in each of the four companies.

Hanson's logic for this demerger was the belief that each company would benefit from greater management focus on improving its operations, profitability and long-term prospects.

After an initial flurry of excitement, reactions from the stock market were unenthusiastic, resulting in reduced share prices for the newly independent companies. After 12 months their combined value had declined to approximately two-thirds that of the group when the demerger announcement was first made. The value of the group had been reduced by billions of pounds. Investors were concerned about the falling share value, as well as an announcement of lower dividends. Analysts, on the other hand, applauded the dividend reduction, saying that previous levels were unsustainable.

One reason for the falling share prices is that the sums of the parts of Hanson were worth less than the whole. This is due to the reverse of the argument which justified Hanson's acquisitions; the demerged group carries multiplied head office costs, and an increased interest and tax burden. Millennium Chemical's profits also shrank as they were exposed to US accounting policies.

However, these declining fortunes could be offset partly by the fact that some of the four companies could be bid targets. Perhaps the most elegant way of combining shareholder value with a culture change would be for the demerged companies to fall victim to takeovers themselves.

Institutional backing is not always guaranteed for management teams with proven track records. Failed bids such as those by Hanson (when it was still in favour) for ICI and Williams Holdings for Racal can be attributed in large part to a lack of institutional support.

The much-publicised failures of companies such as Maxwell, Brent Walker and Coloroll, and smaller ones such as Parkfield, owed much to too-rapid expansion in areas where management was able to bring little new to the acquired businesses. Since their growth was largely debt-financed, the failure to create added value was punished by climbing interest rates. Smaller groups such as Evode and Southern Newspapers suffered hostile bids because of earlier acquisitions which underperformed.

It is essential that acquisition policies are based on sound thinking and proper execution. The improved economic climate of the late 1990s may not punish buyers for poor acquisitions as harshly as these examples, but having the opportunity to cover up for mistakes should not tempt acquirers into becoming carried away by the momentum and excitement of the acquisition process, and failing to stop when warning signs become visible.

Investors look for a clear strategy and a strong prospect of achieving it. They have shown in the cases of Brent Walker and Tace that they are increasingly prepared to intervene and replace an underperforming management team. In the case of Tace, for instance, an institutional revolt led to Graseby's successful hostile bid.

REASONS FOR ACQUISITIONS

Broadly speaking, acquisition strategies can be based on industrial logic (which implies proposed synergies) or on the opportunities for restructuring (which is more cynically described as asset stripping). In most cases the ideal strategy involves a combination of the two: improved sales effectiveness and skills in the market, combined with a reduction in head office costs and the more efficient use of facilities. In practice, most acquirers find it easier to reduce costs than to exploit proposed synergies to increase sales.

Checklist 1 contains four questions which need to be addressed if a company is to be confident that it knows what it is looking for in its acquisition programme. Without satisfactory responses to all four questions, the acquisition may be unsound.

GOOD AND BAD REASONS FOR ACQUISITIONS

Good Reasons

If acquisitions are to be attractive in today's increasingly competitive markets they need to offer at least one (and preferably more) of the following opportunities:

- A brand, technology or reputation that it would be difficult or expensive to replicate, and which is more valuable to the combined business as a whole than it was to the target alone.
- A reduction in the cost of entering a market.
- A more rapid entry into a market when time is of the essence.
- Better exploitation of existing distribution chains or access to new distribution chains.
- Critical mass and management expertise in a new market.
- Genuine synergies which few or no other buyers can match. Examples of genuine synergies are:
  - economies of scale in production of goods or provision of services.
  - rationalisation of resources applied to production, sales or distribution.
- The opportunity to improve on the performance of assets underexploited by weaker previous management.

The point about the presence of other buyers bears elaboration. If

CHECKLIST 1

Strategic Issues for Acquirers to Address

1 What are the acquirer's objectives?
- What are the shareholders' objectives?
- What extra profits can be generated by an enlarged business?
- How are these required returns to be obtained; in which sector and with which resources?
- How do acquisitions fit into the overall strategy?

2 Is acquisition the right approach?
- What are the alternatives to acquiring?
- Are the resources available to carry out the acquisition?
- Could an acquired business be integrated satisfactorily?

3 What are the acquirer's skills?
- What are its core competences?
- What special advantages or skills does it have?
- What resources are available which could be applied to the other business?

4 Why buy *this* target?
- Are the target's assets well understood:
  - products
  - technologies
  - customer base
  - distribution channels
  - brands
  - management skills?
- How can value be added to any of these?
- Are there realistic opportunities for cost reduction?
- Will subsequent asset sales be important?
- Are there better acquisition targets?
- How will the acquirer cope if the proposed synergies do not materialise?

there is competition to buy the target company, the successful bidder will be, more often than not, the one that bids the highest price. Examples to the contrary are more common in continental Europe than in the UK. For instance, Forte lost Cegiva, the Italian hotel group, to a lower bid for political reasons. Bids can only be justified by the benefits to the shareholders of both buyer and seller, so the top bidder must have some special characteristics which make the target more valuable to it than to other bidders.

Such special value can arise in three ways:

Business-related. Economies of scale such as rationalisation of production, use of a single distribution system, brand extension and common procurement. Williams Holdings' rationalisation of the UK paint industry and Redland's rationalisation of European brick production were excellent examples of business-related value being created.

Management-related. Temporary relocation of highly skilled managers with relevant experience can significantly improve the effectiveness of a company's people. Conglomerates such as Hanson, Wassall and TT would also argue that management performance can be greatly enhanced by applying strict disciplines in production and financial control.

Finance-related. Advantages accruing to the acquirer or to the combined group through an improved tax position or an improved capital structure.

Unless the possibility of one or more of these special values exists, it is unlikely that the business' performance will justify the highest bid.

Restructuring companies to create value in these ways is an important process in modern economies. There are management teams that dedicate themselves entirely to extracting value from assets that are underperforming, whatever the sector. A wide range of skills may be required, including reducing the cost of production, rationalising product ranges, removing management layers and taking other tough decisions which previous managers found difficult for intellectual or emotional reasons.

Bad Reasons

Many other reasons are advanced for pursuing particular acquisitions. On occasions some may be sound, but often they result from unclear thinking.

Some examples are:

— "The company needs to diversify."
  - Why not let shareholders do their own diversification? It is cheaper for them to do it and easier to reverse.
— "Our marketing experience in similar markets will be invaluable."
  - How similar? What exactly are we going to do? Who will do it?
— "There is extensive scope for synergy."
  - Easier to claim than to exploit. Quantify it in detail and plan how it will actually be achieved.
— "The market was undervaluing components of the target business."
  - Maybe, but would this still be the case after paying a substantial acquisition premium?
— "If we do not buy it someone else might."
  - Yes, but do we actually want it? What will we do with it? What is its real value to us? Just how much worse a threat is it in somebody else's hands?
— "Our borrowing costs will be lower because the risk will be spread."
  - Possibly, but unless there are other good reasons to buy, this benefit will go to our bankers, not to our shareholders.
— "Today's favourable exchange rates make the acquisition cheap."
  - Why not speculate in foreign currency as opposed to businesses?
— "The City will like it."
  - But will it also like it in the long term?
— "We need to be a billion dollar business."
  - Is this really the case, or just personal aggrandisement?

A SUCCESSFUL EXAMPLE

After a series of warnings and cautionary tales this chapter will close with a successful example of an acquisition-driven market entry strategy – see Case Study 3. Based on good reasons for acquisition, the strategy was devised to achieve its objectives while minimising the inherent risks.

CASE STUDY 3: EMAP: ACQUISITION-DRIVEN MARKET ENTRY STRATEGY

Background

Emap, the Peterborough-based publishing group, operated wholly in the UK until 1990. Its activities included publishing consumer magazines, business-to-business magazines and regional newspapers. The company enjoyed rapid growth in the UK but by 1990 it was running out of domestic growth opportunities. The French market seemed attractive with 86% of French people regularly reading a magazine; it is one of the biggest magazine markets in the world.

A Structured Approach

Emap took a step-by-step approach to market entry.

1   Three-month Secondment to the Market

Kevin Hand, who was to become president of Emap France, spent three months in France perfecting his command of French language and culture, and scouting for opportunities. Emap took the view that the French are very proud of their language and that they expect serious business people to speak it.

2 Joint Venture to Create a Presence and to Learn

In 1990 Emap set up a joint venture vehicle with Bayard Presse, a French publisher. The creation of this presence was in response to what Emap describes as "l'exception française" – France's self proclaimed right (indeed duty) to be different. Emap says this requires a local presence and creates traps for unwary newcomers.

In July 1990, Emap, together with its new partner Bayard Presse, acquired *Le Chasseur Français*, the French monthly country living magazine with a circulation of nearly 600000. At £17.2 million, Emap overpaid for this acquisition. It argues the premium was justified as there were few alternative entry routes, and it established critical mass in France.

3 In-country Management Experience

Another senior Emap manager moved to France; others were regularly involved in the business. The goal was to learn from the French how to run a publishing business in France and to transfer skills between the two operations.

4 Organic Growth from the Newly Established Base

Having created a presence in France, Emap followed up its first acquisition by launching its own magazine titles such as *Peche Pratique*, *Reponses Photo* and *Consolus Plus*. All were in niche areas, but corresponded to markets already well known to the publisher in the UK.

5 Further acquisitions

As Emap had overpaid for *Le Chasseur Français*, several acquisition opportunities were presented by shareholders attracted by a wealthy British acquirer. However, Emap rejected these opportunities, as now that its strategic goals had been achieved its intention was not to overpay again.

After some four years of learning and understanding the market,

Emap felt ready to take on a big acquisition. In June 1994, it spent £92 million on acquiring 28 titles through the acquisition of Éditions Mondiales, a Paris-based publisher. Three other smaller acquisitions (totalling £27 million) accompanied that deal, including France's biggest-selling motoring journal, *l'AutoJournal*.

Éditions Mondiales was a big and inefficient company operating at break-even. Emap had a real struggle to improve profitability and to integrate it into its existing operations. The experience already gained in the French market was essential. If Emap had acquired Éditions Mondiales earlier in its entry strategy, it would possibly not have succeeded.

Emap's next acquisition – the £142 million purchase of *Télé Star*, *Top Santé* and *Télé Star Jeux* (turnover £95 million) in March 1996 – was its biggest, doubling its share of the French consumer magazine market to 16%.

Conclusion

Emap is one of the few British publishing companies to have entered the French market successfully. Emap's management came to understand the market by partnering with a French publisher and by putting people on the ground who got to grips with how the country operates. It was then able to acquire major companies and to integrate them.

4
Finding the Opportunities

UNDERSTANDING THE MARKET

Before pursuing a particular acquisition opportunity within a market it is essential to understand the dynamics of the market and its long-term attractiveness to shareholders. The UK's building societies failed to do this before rushing into the wholesale acquisition of estate agents. This need to understand the market is true for both potential new entrants and for current participants seeking growth either organically or through acquisition.

As well as helping an acquirer decide if it makes sense to acquire in a specific market, the market review may, of course, throw up some potential acquisition targets at the same time.

IDENTIFYING TARGETS

Acquisitions are usually identified through one of the following routes:

- A company puts itself up for sale by contacting other businesses which it thinks may be interested, such as partners, suppliers, customers and competitors; some of these potential acquirers will already have signalled their intention to the prospective seller.
- The company for sale uses an intermediary to find a buyer.
- An intermediary works proactively as marriage broker,

matching a business which is not "officially" for sale to interested partners.

- An acquirer approaches directly a company it already knows with an indication of interest or with a proposition.
- A member of the acquirer's staff uncovers an opportunity through contacts in the market.
- The acquirer conducts a systematic search for acquisition targets.

SYSTEMATIC APPROACH

The AMR/ICME survey confirms the view that acquisitions made on a purely opportunistic basis are more likely to be disappointing in the long run. Figure 4.1 shows the acquirers met their original strategic objectives in only 32% of cases when the acquisition was made on a purely opportunistic basis.

The most successful acquisitions tend to be those that fit within a predetermined strategic plan, although the acquirer may have to react opportunistically when the target company becomes available. Operating units of groups are well advised to establish and agree the criteria for potential acquisitions in their strategic plans so they can react effectively when a business becomes available, and not have to convince a sceptical board of the logic.

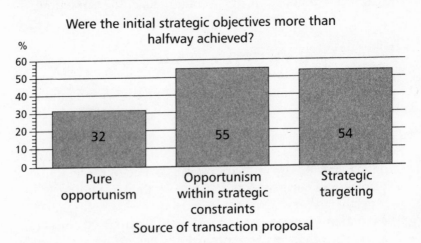

Figure 4.1   *Strategic approach beats opportunism* (*Source:* AMR/ICME survey).

There are few experiences more frustrating for acquirers than buying one company and then finding out that a comparable target was available at a better price, or that a more attractive company may have been available at a similar price. This can happen when management is working with imperfect information, and especially when an opportunity arises suddenly and management believes it has to be grasped quickly.

The lack of available suitable targets can be a major frustration for would-be acquirers. Although seemingly unavailable targets can sometimes be won over, patience is essential. Frustrated acquirers should not rewrite their strategies because a company becomes available if that company has already been judged unacceptable. Benson Group learned this lesson when it opportunistically acquired a diversified group of private companies after declaring automotive and heating to be its core business. Substantial losses led to top management changes and the injection of rescue capital.

A systematic search allows the acquirer to base an acquisition on the quality of fit of the target, as opposed to its availability. Also, a systematic search for the most appropriate opportunities can form a sound base for the due diligence process. A further advantage is to create a more powerful negotiating position: the target company's owners are left in little doubt that the acquirer has a number of choices and is, therefore, less likely to overpay.

The search approach is particularly relevant in fragmented markets or when targets are niche players which are difficult to identify. Any search should be carefully designed to give practical results and to form the basis for effective decision making by acquirers.

SEARCH OBJECTIVES

The objectives of a systematic search are to answer the questions:

- What companies are in the market?
- What are their areas of activity in terms of product range, geography and market segment?
- What are their approximate market shares?
- How good is their management?
- What are their overall strengths and weaknesses?

- How would they fit with the acquirer?
- What are their ownership structures?
- Might they be available, and at what price?

In the first instance, basic information will be required for a large number of businesses. Significantly greater levels of detail will then be required on the potential acquisition targets thrown up by the search. Later, in the due diligence process, even more detail will be obtained, both on the target and its key competitors.

The amount of effort required to research a market for acquisition targets will depend greatly on the characteristics of the desired acquisition. For instance, if the search is limited to large businesses in a single country then the effort required will be less than if it encompasses a wide range of businesses in many countries.

The likelihood of a search revealing an excellent set of candidates will be determined by two factors:

- the appropriateness of the acquisition criteria, or parameters
- the capability of those conducting the search.

PARAMETERS

It is essential that clear parameters are set for an acquisition search. There is no right answer to what the parameters should be; but with appropriate ones in place, the search can be finite and can be monitored effectively. Some examples of parameters for an acquisition search are:

- Geography
    country
    region of operations
- Business
    product
    service offered
- Resources
    machinery types
    technologies
    skills
    facilities

- Size
    - turnover and employee numbers
    - acceptable ranges
- Profitability
    - gross margins
    - operating margins
    - net margins
    - ROCE
    - cash generated
    - acceptable levels
- Ownership
    - plc/subsidiary/private limited company/family company/ partnership etc.
    - acceptable current ownership structure
- Customers
    - key customer groups or industry segments served
- Standards
    - e.g. ISO 9000
- Other
    - as relevant to the industry
- Unacceptable elements
    - machine types
    - technologies
    - skills
    - facilities
    - customer groups.

OUTCOME

Depending on the search parameters and on the sector, approximately 5–15% of the companies screened will be considered sufficiently attractive for subsequent evaluation. Those companies that continue to appear attractive after evaluation should then be approached. Chapter 5 sets out the best methodology to follow during these phases.

If no acquisition results from a search it can be concluded that no appropriate company is available. The sector can then be monitored periodically for developments, and in the meantime resources can be more usefully directed elsewhere. Should an opportunity to acquire arise at a later stage within a sector previously screened, then the acquirer already has an under- standing of the potential targets and can rapidly compare the available company with its competitors.

For example, the European industrial ceramics sector went through a period of consolidation in the late 1980s and early 1990s: many companies were acquired, leaving a handful of significant companies in independent ownership. Subsequent prospective acquirers, having established contact with each of the remaining companies, could take no further action in the sector until an opportunity arose and had to concentrate devel- opment resources elsewhere.

One common reason for attractive acquisition opportunities being passed over is the lack of sufficient knowledge to judge whether or not the opportunity was a good one. Only a system- atic analysis of the sector will provide this knowledge and give a sound basis for proceeding.

ONE-OFF REVIEWS OR CONTINUOUS SCREENING?

A one-off review of a sector is often conducted when time is of the essence. For instance, a comparative framework may be required if one or more targets are unexpectedly identified. Al- ternatively, as in the industrial ceramics example given above, confirmation may be required that no opportunities exist and that resources are best re-directed elsewhere.

A continuous approach to screening and monitoring a sector is best used in an industry with a large number of participants where a series of transactions is proposed.

WHO SHOULD CONDUCT THE SEARCH?

Although conducting an acquisition search may appear to be a simple exercise, it is not. When investigating a highly frag- mented market even experienced specialists cannot guarantee that every company which fits the parameters will be identified. Nonetheless skilled searchers will use sources far wider than standard industry directories and supposedly comprehensive databases.

To be successful, some lateral thinking is required. For example, in some sectors suppliers will have excellent knowledge of the relevant companies, while in others it may be customers who are best informed. Wherever the information lies, it needs to be accessed. Then, to screen the companies, direct contact should be made with each one to find out whether or not it falls within the parameters.

Specialists such as AMR have an approach to acquisition searches that identifies the factors that will be important for each decision and provides the high-quality information required to take those decisions. Before engaging a specialist, find out if it will conduct a market analysis, help with the definition of acquisition criteria, be involved in the selection of a short list, provide advice about the best way to approach a potential target, and subsequent negotiation strategy. Acquisition searches are normally conducted primarily with desk research and telephone interviews. Conducting a number of face-to-face interviews with market participants greatly enhances the value of the search and leads to the best possible results.

To give some indications of the scope of a systematic search, examples from recent searches by AMR are given in Table 4.1. They show the number of businesses screened in each case and the number of businesses that met the acquisition criteria of the potential buyer.

An acquirer's contacts and industry knowledge may be such that the search process can be conducted in-house. However, unless the company's staff are very knowledgeable about the market, it makes sense to use consultants. Specialist consultants are likely to have more experience of interviewing acquisition candidates and it is often easier for a third party to gain information from managers who might be reluctant to speak directly to a potential acquirer.

The use of consultants requires a clear research brief, setting out precisely the work to be carried out by both sides, and the outputs required. Otherwise, especially in fragmented or difficult sectors, there are risks that the results will not come up to

Table 4.1   *Number of companies screened in acquisition searches.*

Sector	Countries	Businesses screened	Of interest
Aerospace	USA	90	6
Industrial textiles	France, Germany, Italy	120	25
Industrial ceramics	Western Europe	140	15
Mining equipment	USA	80	12
Waste treatment	UK	400	18
Air conditioning	UK	300	35
Cotton spinning and processing	UK, France, Germany, Italy	100	22
Engineering software	Germany	80	8
Cable accessories	UK, France, Germany, USA	110	3

Source: AMR

expectations. Consultants can be used in a one-off exercise, or they can monitor a changing sector continuously for the availability of acquisition prospects.

NETWORKS

As well as using contacts among suppliers, customers and others active in target markets, opportunities can be identified by networking among intermediaries. The big accountants are often in touch with businesses seeking an ownership change and venture capitalists will always be looking for an exit route from their investments. Merchant banks can also provide leads.

However, relying on intermediaries to suggest transaction opportunities is rarely satisfactory. Intermediaries will often not be properly focused as they are dealing with numerous potential acquirers. Also, it is necessary for the potential acquirer to re-brief the chosen set of intermediaries on a regular basis to maintain their awareness of the acquirer's acquisition criteria. Experienced acquirers report that at least 100 opportunities thrown up by this route need to be reviewed before an acquisition can be expected to result.

Although most serious acquirers do brief their intermediary networks on their acquisition interests, they also dedicate internal or external resources to a detailed acquisition search.

Case Study 4 describes an acquisition search conducted by AMR on behalf of a privatised water utility, which had taken the strategic decision to increase its share of the UK liquid waste business. The market was highly fragmented, but as consolidation had begun, time was of the essence.

CASE STUDY 4: UK WASTE MANAGEMENT ACQUISITION SEARCH

Acquirer

Privatised water utility, with a limited operation in liquid waste transport, treatment and disposal.

Objectives

1 Review market structure, growth prospects, entry barriers and opportunities in each selected geographic region.
2 Identify acquisition targets.

Parameters

Targets were sought that fell within the following parameters:

- involved in the transport of liquid industrial waste
- involved in the treatment of liquid industrial waste
- profitable, or at least breaking even
- preferably owner-managed
- ownership of, or guaranteed access to, licensed disposal sites
- minimum size: five owned tankers
- manufacturing customer base preferred
- industrial cleaning excluded.

Method

1 All relevant companies were identified using industrial and local directories, contact with major customers and regulators.

2 A database of 400 potential targets was developed.
3 Each one of the potential targets was contacted to ascertain whether they matched the acquisition parameters.
4 Those companies that failed to meet basic size, capability and service criteria were eliminated.
5 A first short list was reviewed with the client, and targets were prioritised. The top 15 companies were selected.
6 Face-to-face interviews were arranged with the shareholders and senior management (they were often the same) of the 15 companies with the best fit. These meetings allowed AMR to develop detailed profiles on each one as an acquisition target. Information already obtained was confirmed and significant further detail was added about each operation. The market position of each company was confirmed and the aspirations of shareholders, including their willingness to join forces with a major company, were investigated. Client anonymity was retained during this phase.
7 The results were reviewed with the client. Three companies were rejected as unsuitable acquisition targets. (One of them was treating five times more waste than the capacity of its facility, which was situated over a disused mineshaft.)
8 Introductions were made to the owners of 12 of the targeted companies. The manner of each introduction was tailored to the shareholders' circumstances and aspirations.

Result

On the basis of the information obtained and the relationships created with the 12 companies introduced to the acquiring group, eight targets chose to enter into discussions, and two were acquired. This result was achieved in a competitive market with a number of other players simultaneously seeking to consolidate the sector.

The water company continued to grow the business through organic means. Meanwhile, the database of potential targets allowed new opportunites to be evaluated as they arose over the following years as industry consolidation continued.

Conclusion

This case study highlights a number of issues:

- The search consultant's approach should be designed to identify the factors that will be important for each decision and to provide high-quality information on which to take these decisions – market definition, acquisition criteria, selection of short list, nature of approaches to be made and input to negotiation strategy.
- The use of face-to-face interviews to supplement telephone interviews and desk research gives the best possible results.
- Information should be sought from market participants with a knowledge of potential candidate companies and from the targets themselves.

THE NEXT STEP

Although often frustratingly slow, finding the best company to acquire can be the easy part of the exercise. This guide will now consider the issues surrounding the process of approaching and evaluating the target company.

5
Making the Approach

Making an acquisition approach can appear to be much more complex and difficult than it really is. The golden rule is to take great care to ensure that the best possible way is found to broach the subject. Very often this preparation can make or break a relationship and hence a deal. If the management team of a potential acquirer is uncomfortable with the process of investigating how the approach should be made and then making it, a third party can be used.

FORMULATING THE BEST APPROACH

Questions that need to be raised when considering the best approach are:

- Who are the shareholders?
- What is the balance of power between the shareholders?
- Are there any other significant stakeholders who should be involved, such as joint venture partners?
- Would a direct approach be preferred to one through an intermediary?
- How disguised or blunt should the approach be?
- From which management level in the potential acquirer should the approach be made?
- For cross-border deals, is language an issue?

It is rare that a blunt approach – "We want to buy your business"

– is successful. This is particularly so outside the UK and North America. In many countries, including much of continental Europe and Asia, selling a business is considered to be an admission of failure, whereas in the Anglo-Saxon business community it is more likely to be considered as a major success. One effective way to gauge the style of approach that is most likely to succeed is to enter into discussions on subjects such as a joint venture or technology transfer, creating a working relationship before addressing the issue of ownership of the target business.

METHODS

Possible methods of making an approach include:

- direct approach
- using a common third party, such as institutional shareholders or non-executive directors
- anonymous approach through an intermediary.

The direct approach can be the simplest. However, it is essential that the approach is made in person and in the right context. Surprisingly, there have been cases where Anglo-Saxon managers have communicated a desire to acquire foreign companies by fax. Rebuttal is almost inevitable.

If there is a third party known to both sides, this channel can be the best one to use. The third party will already have a clear idea of how the approach should be made and what the key sensitivities might be.

The use of intermediaries provides independent feedback on the aspirations of the shareholders and can avoid embarrassment. In some countries it may be best to use a local, as long as they have acceptable credentials with the target company. If an intermediary has been used successfully to evaluate the target during an acquisition search, a positive relationship should have been formed. The intermediary can then use this relationship to make the approach and introduce the potential acquirer on a suitable basis.

LIKELY REACTIONS

It is useful to consider some of the likely reactions that a target may have.

From a Group

A potential acquirer can expect a balanced and relatively unemotional response from a group to an acquisition approach concerning a subsidiary. The nature of the response and the willingness to discuss disposal will depend on the extent to which the subsidiary is considered to be a core business. Unless a strategic decision has just been taken that the subsidiary would be available, a typical response is that "every business is available at the right price".

This attitude reflects the normal clarity of purpose of a quoted group: to maximise shareholder value. If group management believes that the long-term prospects of the business are less attractive than the benefit of achieving a likely offer price, it should sell. If a quoted group is keen to progress a deal, it will typically release some outline financial and commercial information. An indicative offer would then be expected before any more information is released.

From Owner-Managers

The reactions of owner-managers can be very varied. The key to success is understanding their philosophy and their aspirations. The classic point at which owner-managed businesses are sold is when the founder approaches retirement and there is no obvious succession. However, if no consideration has previously been given to sale there is a danger that owner-managers may be excited by any form of approach as it can be the first step towards making them millionaires. In these cases their perceptions of the value of the business can become unrealistic.

In practice, many owner-managers are very wary of any approach. They fear the damage that may be caused to their business by new owners, such as trusted employees being fired or business ideals being ignored. Also, many owner-managers fear that any potential acquirer may just be a potential competitor in disguise. Owner-managers tend to be more acutely aware of what they stand to lose by entering into negotiation with a potential acquirer than the salaried employees of a group. They need to be treated with great sensitivity.

From Passive Family Shareholders

Passive family shareholders often have the interests of the current management close to heart. If not, they are likely to be willing sellers. In cases where second-generation shareholders control the business there can be important differences of outlook and aspirations between key shareholders. Some of these shareholders' views may also be at odds with the views of operational management. These circumstances can lead to a positive reaction to any approach as it can lead to a resolution of differences.

However, in such cases an approach to the shareholders via their operational management may very well be rejected: management may fear for their jobs, or they may be seeking an MBO. The disadvantage of trying to buy a business with a wide and unco-ordinated shareholder base is that they will often find it difficult to agree on whether to sell the business, let alone at what price.

From Venture Capitalists

Venture capitalists make an equity investment in a business with a view to realising a profit on the sale of their equity stake after 3–5 years. For this reason venture capitalists are always interested in an "exit" from a company in which they have invested.

However, venture capitalists set very demanding targets for their investments and will always be seeking a high price. For example, in 1990 venture capitalists paid £3 million for a 20% stake in C-Com, a mobile telephone designer and manufacturer valuing the company at £15 million. Despite high hopes, the company did not meet its growth and profit targets. In 1992 Matra Communications offered £8 million for the whole business but the venture capitalists were not prepared to sell at a loss. In retrospect this was a poor decision: C-Com was sold to another trade buyer within one year, on the verge of liquidation, for less than £1 million.

There are plenty of more positive examples of venture capitalists making annual returns of 30–50% on their investments. Well-known examples include Reed Packaging and Solartron.

THE NEXT STEP

Having considered how to make an approach and how well it is likely to be received, detailed thought must be given to how the potential benefit to the acquirer should be evaluated.

6
Evaluating the Potential Benefit to the Acquirer

EVALUATION

Shareholders in acquiring companies can fail to benefit for at least three reasons:

- the acquisition was not entirely appropriate in the first place and did not increase the value of the combined businesses
- the acquisition was less attractive than at first believed as problems associated with the business became clear only after control was taken
- the acquisition was a good idea, but too much was paid and the benefits went to the seller's shareholders.

The most frequent reason why shareholders of acquirers fail to benefit is the third: overpaying. Figure 6.1, from the AMR/ICME survey, shows the direct correlation between acquirers paying too much and the acquisition failing.

CREATING SHAREHOLDER VALUE

The value created for the acquirer's shareholders is defined as follows:

1 Value created for buyer = Maximum price that should be paid to seller − Actual price paid to seller.

2 Maximum that should by paid to seller = Stand-alone value of the acquisition + Value created by acquisition.

Derived from Rappaport: *Creating Shareholder Value*

VALUE-CREATION POTENTIAL

Issues to be aware of when judging the value-creation potential of an acquisition to shareholders are:

- The stand-alone price (the independent value of the business, not taking any synergies into account) will generally be the lowest price a seller will consider.
- A forced sale may, however, cause the seller to go below this price (retirement or short-term liquidity problems may lead to this).
- New entrants to a sector will often pay a premium to obtain access to a market.
- A buyer who is particularly well placed to benefit from the position of the combined business can afford to pay more than less well-placed competitors.
- A buyer who can deliver real synergies is even better off.
- An owner-managed business may require more investment than a subsidiary of a group to bring its systems into line with those of the acquirer.

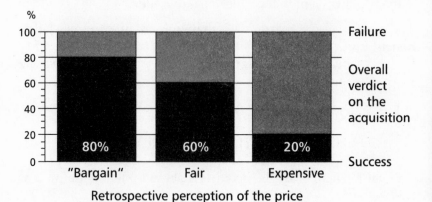

Figure 6.1 *"Do not overpay"* (*Source:* AMR/ICME survey).

- A favourable tax position can provide a significant advantage to certain buyers.
- There is much to be gained or lost in negotiation and often the price paid will reflect the parties' respective negotiating skills as much as other issues.

Chapter 8 contains a description of the valuation methods commonly applied to acquisitions. Standard investment appraisal techniques based on discounted cash flow should be applied in all cases, possibly supplemented by other techniques as appropriate. However, the value of using more than one approach will be realised only if the reasons for their differing results are properly understood.

Figure 6.2 highlights the necessity of proving the actual value of synergies.

The maximum price the acquirer should pay is the most that can be paid while still earning the normal rate of return on the transaction. The ways in which acquisition can create value were discussed in Chapters 2 and 3.

The golden rule is not to negotiate away the synergies, although in practice this is difficult. The acquirer's ability not to give away the benefit of those synergies will depend on the

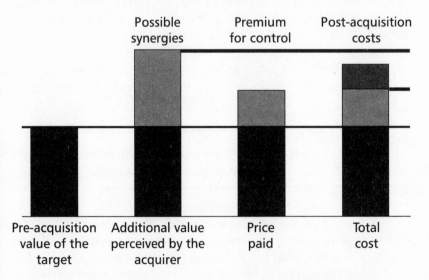

Figure 6.2　*Working out an acceptable premium (Source: AMR/ICME survey).*

relative negotiating position of the parties. The overpriced deal is one where synergies have been conceded. As synergies often fail to reach the full amount anticipated, many acquirers find that they have paid too much for a set of promises or expectations that could not be delivered.

Examples of cases where an acquirer may be prepared to pay a premium include:

- high barriers to entry in a new territory
- the inherent difficulties and time required to achieve a worthwhile market share by organic growth
- the need to catch up on technology developments quickly.

ASSESSING ATTRACTIVENESS

Acquisitions are simply one of the weapons in the business development armoury. Accordingly, standard capital investment appraisal procedures should be applied to acquisitions, involving the estimation of post-tax cash flows, discounted at the acquirer's cost of capital. These are briefly dealt with in Chapter 8.

Businesses are best assessed by breaking them down into their component parts. If a group is being reviewed, each company should be assessed on its own merits. Companies should be broken down by product or service lines.

It is also useful to consider the value of each element of each business under two headings:

- the value of the ongoing business
- the new value that will be added.

The new value to be added includes benefits from economies of scale, rationalisation and improved management skills. The buyer's initial negotiating position should be that these will not be paid for, except for the ongoing business.

Potential acquirers should use standard appraisal tools to review the position and prospects of the target business. In almost every case a basic SWOT (strengths, weaknesses, opportunities and threats) analysis of the target, or its component parts, can

Strengths	Weaknesses
Current strengths of the business for which the acquirer is prepared to pay. These attributes are methods of generating profits now and in the future and of creating value.	Current weaknesses of the business. Often they can be overcome, at a cost, by management action or investment. Ideally, the acquirer will have skills and resources which can counter key weaknesses; these are some of the much talked about synergies.
Opportunities	Threats
Areas of growth or opportunities for future growth, given suitable management action or investment. Again the acquirer should bring skills and resources which will make some of these opportunities easier to achieve.	Issues beyond the control of the company which could damage its position and performance. It is important to assess the scale of these threats and the likelihood of them occurring. It is important also to consider what actions can be taken to mitigate the impact of the threats.

Figure 6.3   *Using SWOT analysis to assess attractiveness.*

form a useful basis for evaluation. Care should be taken to identify the salient issues under each of the four headings set out in Figure 6.3.

SELLERS DO BETTER

Assuming that the acquisition does create value, how this is carved up between the buyer and the seller is determined by the competitiveness of the market for such companies and the negotiating skills of the two sides. If there are numerous potential purchasers, then the seller's shareholders will receive more of the benefit as the price will be bid up. For example, William Low's shareholders benefited by £93 million by the entry of Sainsbury into the bidding for the company in competition with Tesco. Sainsbury's reported objective was less to acquire William Low itself than to make its rival pay out more.

CASE STUDY 5: A COMPANY IS WORTH WHAT A BUYER IS PREPARED TO PAY

William Low

Tesco management had been watching the situation at William Low for some years when the Scottish supermarket chain's share price fell to a new low in the early months of 1994.

After hard negotiating Tesco made an initial offer of 225p per share for William Low in July 1994. This valued the company at £154 million. Advised by Barings, William Low accepted this offer on the basis that it represented a value higher than justified as an independent company. That would have been the end of the story, if J. Sainsbury had not intervened.

Rivalry

Tesco is Sainsbury's arch rival. Sainsbury's management considered that Tesco was getting a bargain at £154 million. In order to make life more difficult for Tesco they had to overcome their long-standing aversion to hostile deals.

J. Sainsbury launched a hostile bid at 305p per share topping Tesco's offer by 35.5% and valuing William Low at £210 million. It was widely believed that Sainsbury's only motive for entering the bidding was to drive up the price for Tesco. However, Tesco's advisers recognised that Sainsbury would not have entered without willingness to take the business on.

Tesco's management was convinced that their greater presence and experience in the region put them in the best position to obtain maximum value out of William Low. They decided to make a second offer that still made commercial sense, but which was also high enough to discourage Sainsbury's return to the bidding.

Tesco's second offer of 360p topped its first by no less than 60%, valuing the Scottish supermarket operator at £247 million. This made it difficult for Sainsbury's to justify another bid, and Tesco completed the acquisition.

	Price per share	Value	% increase
Initial Tesco offer	225 p	£154 m	–
Sainsbury's bid	305 p	£210 m	35.5%
Tesco's second offer	360 p	£247 m	60%

Conclusions

- A buyer in exclusive negotiations has every chance of obtaining a better deal.
- The shareholders of a seller are better off if there are competing buyers.
- The value of a company is whatever a buyer is prepared to pay for it. In this case, William Low was worth £93 million more to Tesco than its original offer had indicated.
- There is no rule as to what price a company is worth or will be sold for.

In the 1990s few acquirers are willing to pay the seller's shareholders a significant premium for benefits that they will bring or for value that only the acquirer can add or create. For example, if an acquirer can unlock the target's distribution problem, the future benefit of this advantage should go to the buyer's shareholders. This should be reflected by omission of the expected improvement from a discounted cash flow calculation of the value of the existing company. Projections for profits to be made by unproven products and services are nowadays also usually stripped out of any valuation appraisal.

Historical evidence suggests that, on average, shareholders of quoted companies receive a significant benefit from agreeing to their company being acquired. The buyers' shareholders have usually received a smaller benefit, or even suffered losses. Studies that asked managers whether acquisitions have been worthwhile and those examining share price performance indicate that buyers have too often paid more than they should have, and that in many cases they have actually diminished the value of their shareholders' investment.

This evidence is based on quoted transactions where premiums in the range of 20–50% over pre-offer market prices are common and where one might expect to find a very competitive market for company control. This does, of course, leave open the possibility that more favourable conditions for acquisition are to be found in the less open market for unquoted companies and businesses that are subsidiaries or divisions.

In fragmented markets the sort of systematic search described in Chapter 4 can allow acquirers to uncover potential bargains in the unquoted sector. Not every seller will be aware of the full value of their business to the acquirer.

RELATIVE SIZE

The relative size of the target to the acquirer can be an important issue. The acquisition of a relatively small business will incur many of the same transaction costs as a larger deal. Also, it may not be considered worthy of as much operational management attention from the acquirers as larger businesses, at least until it starts to underperform; at this point it can suck up significant amounts of management time and attention for little return.

Very large acquisitions, on the other hand, bring the potential

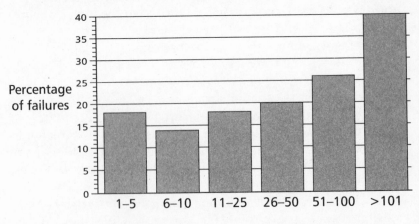

Figure 6.4 *Consider your target's relative size (Source: AMR/ICME survey).*

of a substantial up-side, but they are particularly dangerous when things start to go wrong. The disastrous acquisition of VG Instruments by Fisons is just one example.

The AMR/ICME survey found that the ideal acquisition size is 6–10% that of the acquirer. This is illustrated in Figure 6.4.

NEED FOR DETAIL

Detailed strategic thinking is required to evaluate the potential benefit to the acquirer. Chapter 7 focuses on some very necessary tactical detail: due diligence.

7
Due Diligence

The term due diligence refers to the process of detailed investigation of a proposed acquisition target. A thorough due diligence process looks at all aspects of a company's operations: its positioning and prospects in the market, the way it produces the product and services it sells, its culture and management policies, its assets, its financial resources, its contractual relationships and so on.

TYPES OF DUE DILIGENCE

There are three main types of due diligence. Each requires a separate and thorough approach. They are:

- commercial
- financial
- legal.

Table 7.1 sets out and compares these and other forms of due diligence.

Some of the types of due diligence described in the table can be combined. For example, environmental and legal can be combined (if independent environmental consultants are hired it is essential that they are well insured), IT and financial can be combined and acquirers often ask commercial due diligence specialists to investigate the market's view of the target's management quality.

Table 7.1   *Types of due diligence and outputs.*

Types	Focus of enquiries	Results sought
Main forms		
Commercial	Competitive position, quality of key relationships	Sustainability of future profits, formulation of strategy for the combined business, input to valuation
Financial	Validation of historical information, review of management and systems	Financial analysis, basis for valuation
Legal	Contractual agreements, problem-spotting	Warranties and indemnities, validation of all existing contracts, acquisition agreement
Other forms		
Tax	Existing tax levels, liabilities and arrangements	Opportunities to optimise position of combined business
Environmental	Liabilities arising from sites and processes	Potential liabilities, nature and cost of actions to limit them
Management and culture	Culture, management quality, organisational structure	Identification of key integration issues, outline of new structure for the combined businesses
IT	Performance and adequacy of current systems	Feasibility of integrating systems; associated costs
Operational/ technical	Production techniques, validity of current technology	Technical threats; sustainability of current methods; opportunities for improvement; investment requirements
Patent	Validity, duration and protection of patents	Expiration; impact and cost

INFORMATION PROVIDED BY THE TARGET

Careful consideration should obviously be given to the information provided by the target during the due diligence phase. This information becomes available in increasingly useful amounts as the acquisition process advances – particularly if the target recognises that the acquirer is tapping its own independent sources. It is useful for the acquirer to suggest that the advisers who are conducting commercial due diligence also meet with the top management of the seller, as this provides insights into the business from a different angle and can generate further commercially valuable information.

In auction-style bids the seller may set up a "data room". With photocopying normally not allowed in the data room, the due diligence team rushes to copy out as much detail of key documents as possible and then reconstruct them for analysis back at their own premises.

Various precautions can be built into the purchase agreement itself: disclosures, warranties, retentions, deferred or contingent payments. These are hammered out during negotiations, on the basis of the detailed understanding of the business which is developed during due diligence. However, experienced dealmakers know that the best sale and purchase agreements are those that are never referred to again, let alone in court (these legal protections are referred to in more detail in Chapter 10).

Before the mid 1980s, most due diligence programmes focused exclusively on financial and legal aspects. The more astute acquirers were already making increasing use of commercial due diligence, and in 1987 an event took place which was to persuade many more acquirers to do the same. In that year Ferranti, a well-respected British defence electronics company, acquired the American firm International Signal Controls (ISC). In part, it was persuaded to do so by the claims of ISC about contracts with a number of key government customers outside the USA. Ferranti took no steps to check the validity of these claims, and neither did its advisers. Some major contracts turned out to be false and two years later Ferranti fell into the hands of the liquidators, sunk by a massive hole in its balance sheet.

The affair led to one of the big accounting firms settling out of court for tens of millions of pounds. Figure 7.1 tracks the demise of Ferranti following the ISC deal.

Had the quality of ISC's customer relationships been investigated by Ferranti during commercial due diligence, this plunge into losses and eventual liquidation need not have happened.

It is, therefore, best to recognise the areas of potential risk in advance. One of the most effective risk reducers prior to commitment to an acquisition is commercial due diligence.

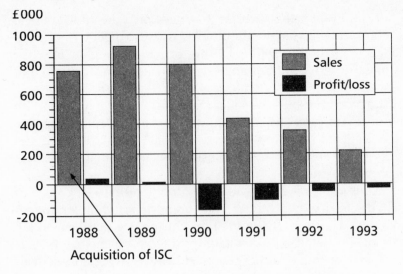

Figure 7.1   *Impact of the ISC acquisition on Ferranti.*

COMMERCIAL DUE DILIGENCE

Commercial due diligence consists of a thorough review of the sector in which the target operates, including competitors, customers, distributors, suppliers and other relevant parties. Commercial due diligence should also provide a thorough review of the target itself and any joint venture or other partners.

The results may validate the information already provided by the target company and they may confirm the potential acquirer's perception of the business. Alternatively, they may sound warning bells. The investigation produces an understanding of the overall market situation, how competitive it is, who the key players are and how successful they are. It generates specific information on the performance of the target – including the subjective views of the other players in the market on the target company.

An essential element of any commercial due diligence exercise will be the analysis of the quality of customer relationships. In particular, former customers should be interviewed. A commercial due diligence specialist will identify all the key relationships that the target has with other companies and review them in

Figure 7.2   *Areas of investigation during commercial due diligence.*

detail. Figure 7.2 sets out the main areas of possible investigation, depending on the nature of the target company.

ROLES OF COMMERCIAL AND FINANCIAL DUE DILIGENCE

Commercial due diligence complements other forms of investigation, particularly financial due diligence. Figure 7.3 shows the roles of financial and commercial due diligence and the relationship between them. As it is now increasingly recognised that these roles are complementary, investigating accountants are often keen to co-operate with commercial due diligence specialists. Although the investigating accountants can in some cases conduct some commercial due diligence work themselves, they are typically limited in their approach and often unable to make the same type of enquiry as a commercial due diligence specialist or a strategy house.

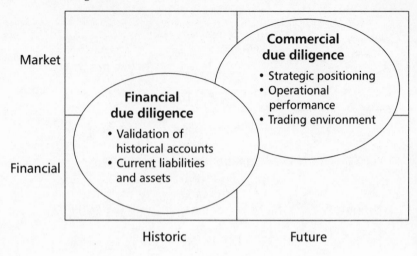

Figure 7.3   *Two complementary roles of commercial and financial due diligence.*

BENEFITS OF COMMERCIAL DUE DILIGENCE

The major benefits of conducting commercial due diligence are:

- historical financial information can be interpreted in the light of current and likely future events
- threats from competitors and new entrants can be identified and assessed
- customer dissatisfactions and unfavourable purchasing trends can be identified
- other external influences such as changes in regulations can be identified and assessed
- forecasts and valuation models can be verified
- the post-acquisition integration tasks and challenges can be understood
- the real, as opposed to the stated, reason for sale can be identified.

Case Study 6 is a typical example of a due diligence exercise carried out by AMR. The investigation was conducted without the knowledge of the target company.

CASE STUDY 6: COMMERCIAL DUE DILIGENCE IN ELECTRONICS

Objective

To investigate a UK-listed engineering group which had a low share price and dissatisfied institutional shareholders. Although the group suffered from numerous management problems, it appeared to hold a leading position in various growth sectors of markets for environmental electronic controls, instrumentation and engineered products.

Method

Personal meetings were held with the directors of each of the subsidiary companies in the UK and USA. Interviews were also held with former employees, competitors, customers and ex-customers of the target group. All of this work was conducted within three weeks on a "no-names" basis; in fact, the existence of a potential acquirer was not disclosed.

Findings

Head Office

Head office costs were disproportionately high compared to staff numbers and compared to any value added. The chief executive's habit of dining and entertaining at Ascot helped to inflate costs. Line management had very little respect for central staff.

Subsidiary 1

The candidate company's strong position in key markets for specialist instrumentation and monitoring systems was confirmed.

No significant competitor had managed to enter this subsidiary's highly regulated market, due to significant barriers to entry. The

Environmental Protection Agency, the US regulator, recognised the company as the leading US supplier in the field.

Subsidiary 2

A long-term threat was identified to this subsidiary's position in the area of specific mechanical devices. Electronic technology was emerging and was likely to substitute the mature mechanical alternative. Nonetheless the mechanical devices were expected to suffer only a slow decline in market share due to the conservativeness of buyers and the way in which the devices are specified.

Subsidiary 3

A major threat from headstrong and disaffected management was identified at this remote subsidiary. The meeting with management revealed that their relationship with head office had been soured by the rejection of two proposed MBOs. The antagonisms (which even led to rumoured threats to burn down the subsidiary's manufacturing facility) made it very unlikely that the group would be able to exploit the subsidiary's technology in new territories and markets.

Subsidiary 4

Long-term threats to this highly cash-generative mechanical engineering business were revealed, although earnings in the medium term were confirmed as being secure. The performance of the business in the USA was identified as very weak due to under-motivated management and an inappropriate distribution structure.

Subsidiary 5

Formerly a market leader in testing equipment, this subsidiary needed new management to rekindle growth. A joint venture partner of this subsidiary, with excellent leading-edge technology, was keen to be acquired.

Outcome

The transaction proceeded and the following actions were immediately taken:

- Subsidiary 3 was rapidly sold to its management, before they could cause any further damage.
- The joint venture partner of subsidiary 5 was rapidly purchased at an attractive price, creating the basis for growth.

Benefits to the Bidder

Benefits to the bidder of conducting commercial due diligence were:

- The value of each subsidiary was fully understood before negotiations began.
- No surprises awaited the acquirer once control was taken.
- Organisational and commercial changes were accurately planned in advance.
- It was clear where stable revenue streams could be expected, and areas of threat to profits in the short, medium and long term were identified.
- Those areas of the business where major investment or support would be required were highlighted, and it was decided in advance which parts of the business should be sold.
- Institutional investors were prepared to back the deal due to the quality of understanding of the targets' businesses and a positive post-acquisition plan.

THE ACQUIRER'S VIEW

Acquirers themselves typically cite two basic reasons for conducting commercial due diligence:

1 To ensure that they avoid paying too much by understanding the true commercial and strategic position of the target. A very

useful question to ask is: "Why is the business for sale?" Owners are often better at spotting the best time to sell than buyers are at understanding when to buy. For example, Smith & Nephew's £126 million acquisition of Loptest in 1988 was undermined by changes in US government regulations; the business was eventually sold in 1994 for only £11 million.

2 Commercial due diligence prepares them for the problems and opportunities they will find in the business. This allows them to plan integration actions in advance and decide how to counter the problems which have been identified and how to act rapidly to exploit the opportunities for growth.

Commercial due diligence is an essential step towards ensuring that the shareholders actually benefit from the transaction. Acquirers are increasingly turning to specialists to conduct commercial due diligence, as they have the investigative skills to uncover problems. At the same time they have the advantage of being independent and their enquiries can be kept discreet. Commercial due diligence is an invaluable tool for management who appreciate that an ill-conceived acquisition can break a career.

FINANCIAL DUE DILIGENCE

As noted at the start of this chapter, financial due diligence is one of the three essential elements of any due diligence investigation. Its importance has long been recognised by acquirers, and consequently it is covered in detail in other texts. Checklist 2 outlines the key issues to be addressed.

CHECKLIST 2

Financial Due Diligence

1 Accounting policies, accounting systems and management information

Consider whether the accounting policies adopted by the company:

- satisfy the national Financial Reporting Standards
- are reasonably prudent and commercially acceptable for the particular business. They should not depart from the fundamental accounting concepts of "going concern", "accruals", "prudence" and "consistency" in terms of time, and policies adopted by the majority of other companies in the same industry.

Consider the adequacy of management accounting:

- when and what information is produced and to whom.

Other reports and systems to be reviewed include:

- stock recording and control
- evaluation of stock and work in progress
- sales order/invoicing system
- purchase control
- debtor and creditor control
- payroll.

Is there consideration and documentation of major decisions, particularly capital expenditure? What criteria are used?

Is there adequate segregation of duties and do adequate authority limits exist?

2 Trading results

For each company and business unit, prepare summarised profit and loss accounts on a historic basis.

Consider the impact of exceptional factors (exchange rate fluctuations, industrial disputes, rationalisation costs, insurance claims, etc.).

Calculate appropriate ratios and obtain and verify, where appropriate, explanations for significant variances over time and differences from sector norms.

Enquire as to any significant transactions with related companies (not being subsidiary or associated companies), for instance "family companies" of major shareholders, etc., not covered by the terms of reference.

Consider whether all income and expenditure are in their correct years.

3 Cash flow statements

Confirm that the cash flow statement (formerly the statement of source and application of funds) has correctly been prepared. Review the reconciliation between operating profit and cash flows from operating activities.

Confirm that cash flows arising from non-trading items (i.e. investing and financing activities) have been correctly reflected in the statement.

Consider the cash generating ability of the business.

4 Assets and liabilities

General

Obtain explanations for significant fluctuations in balance sheet items over the period.

Tangible fixed assets

Ascertain the basis on which tangible fixed assets are included in the balance sheets and note any major revaluations that have been made.

Schedule principal changes in tangible fixed assets; obtain particulars of main capital additions during the period and verify these (together with other major items) where practicable.

Obtain details of all fixed assets held under hire purchase agreements, finance leases and operating leases.

Obtain details of significant intangible fixed assets. Review amortisation policy.

Investments

Obtain details and valuations of all investments.

Check the reasonableness of any interest and dividends received.

Stocks and work in progress

Summarise stocks and work in progress at balance sheet dates and review their valuations.

Analyse the principal trade debtors at the last balance sheet date and also using the latest available information.

Establish whether debts are factored or incurred.

Ensure prepayments are fairly stated and calculated consistently throughout the period.

Cash

For all bank accounts obtain:

• bank certificates and reconciliations
• details of cheque signatories.

Obtain details of borrowing facilities and security held by bank/ lenders.

Review procedures for recording cash. Scan main cash books for large unusual or recurring items: obtain details if necessary.

Creditors

Ascertain:

- supplier (indicating main products supplied)
- age.

Review creditors and accruals to ensure they are properly stated and complete.

Schedule hire purchase and leasing obligations.

Intercompany Transactions

Ensure intercompany accounts reconcile and consider impact of reconciling items.

Consider the accounting treatment of any large intercompany transactions.

Provisions

Schedule principal and needed changes in provisions over the period and reconcile with profit and loss charges.

Contingent liabilities

Review all contingent liabilities and discuss them with management.

If necessary, contact the company's solicitors re contingent liabilities. Consider any outstanding claims and litigation.

5 Taxation

Examine tax computations for the last six years (or period covered by the report, if greater):

- Summarise computations for the period, including draft computations.
- Inspect correspondence with the Inland Revenue.
- Analyse the tax charged to profit and loss account; schedule outstanding tax liabilities.
- Identify adjustments.

Examine provision for deferred taxation:

- the company's accounting policy for deferred taxation
- details of all liabilities to deferred taxation whether or not provided in the accounts
- recompute the provision for any change in the basis of accounting for depreciation or any valuation of assets.

Reconcile overall tax charge with accounts and confirm that the charge in the profit and loss account is properly stated.

Where group relief has been claimed/surrendered check that:

- payments have been correctly made or provided for
- there are no arrangements (including options) for either company to cease to be a member of the group.

If a company is or has been a "close" company:

- obtain copies of any clearances
- agree with the company's taxation advisers the procedure for obtaining clearances for the remaining periods.

Confirm that control of overseas subsidiaries is exercised overseas and that no UK tax liabilities arise on the profits not provided for in the accounts.

Consider future tax liabilities of the company:

- disallowance of trading losses or surplus ACT (advance corporation tax) on change of ownership or a change in the nature or conduct of trade
- ACT liability on repayments of capital or of bonus issues
- large recurring disallowable items
- double taxation relief with losses, group relief, ACT on foreign income
- availability of "small companies rate" for corporation tax.

Determine special taxation provisions on reorganisation.

Calculate potential taxation liabilities not provided or disclosed in accounts.

Consider warranties and indemnities to be included.

Determine vulnerability to PAYE or to other special investigations.

Consider matters relating to potential VAT liabilities:
- examine VAT returns and payments for the past two years
- "surcharge liability notice" served on the company
- penalties incurred due to "serious misdeclaration"
- potential liability for such a penalty.

Consider share schemes for benefit of directors or employees:

- approved Share Option Schemes
- approved Savings Related Share Option Schemes
- approved Profit Sharing Schemes
- non-approved Share Options.

Consider potential liabilities under "controlled foreign companies" legislation.

Assess liabilities through tax avoidance schemes.

Consider extraction of profits or funds giving rise to back duty investigation.

Consider residual liabilities to DLT.

6 Insurance

Determine insurance cover at the latest balance sheet date.

Confirm the adequacy of current cover, particularly in the USA.

7 Pensions

Obtain a copy of:

- trust deed
- rules booklet
- latest accounts
- actuarial valuation report.

Determine eligibility conditions for membership of employees; contribution rates; Inland Revenue approved; whether contracted-out.

Determine how assets are invested. Calculate how the value compares with the value of past service liabilities.

Supplied by BDO Stoy Hayward

LEGAL DUE DILIGENCE

Legal due diligence is the other essential element of due diligence. Chapter 10 sets out the role of the lawyer and how the law can be used to protect the buyer, and outlines the use of warranties and indemnities. Checklist 3 overleaf shows the key issues to cover in legal due diligence.

CHECKLIST 3

Legal Due Diligence

Constitution/Ownership/Status

1   Up-to-date constitutional documents. Does the corporate vendor have power to sell its shares in Target? Are there any restrictions in Target's Articles to the transfer of shares?
2   Details of the authorised and issued share capital.
3   Details of shareholders (including capacity in which they hold shares and any dissenting or untraceable shareholders).
4   Shareholders' agreements (if any).
5   Organisational chart identifying Target's group structure and current directors of each group entity.
6   Options or encumbrances over Target's share capital?
7   Are any assets used by Target owned otherwise than by Target?
8   Are any of Target's assets encumbered or other than in its possession?
9   Are any of the vendors or persons closely connected to them, party to or interested in or entitled to any contracts, loans, intellectual property rights, assets, competitive business or claims of, to, by, against or used by Target?
10 Is Target solvent? Are any insolvency proceedings pending?

Main Contracts

1   Copies of all manufacturing, joint venture, partnership, agency, distributorship, licensing, supply, franchising, outsourcing agreements and standard contracts for sale of goods/supply of services.
2   Details of all major customers and suppliers. Any adverse change in relationships?
3   Copies of all contracts relating to Target's sale/purchase of companies/business/assets in last six years.
4   Copies of loan/credit agreements and related security/guarantee documentation.

5   Bank account details and mandates. Does the acquisition require bank's consent?
6   Details of any major or exercisable change of control of Target.
7   Detail of non-compliance with any contracts.
8   Is Target a party to any non-arm's length arrangement?
9   Has Target given a guarantee or indemnity of any third party's obligations?
10 Are any of Target's contracts subject to avoidance under insolvency legislation?
11 Are any contracts dependent on compliance with British Standards or other special accreditations?

Accounts/Financial Position

1   Audited accounts for last three years.
2   Any management/internal accounts prepared subsequently.
3   Other documents relating to the financial/trading position of the Target since last accounting date. Accountants' report?
4   Any material adverse change since date of last audited accounts?
5   Any bad or doubtful debts?
6   Are stocks adequate, excessive, unusable etc.?
7   Is Target's plant and equipment in good condition/does it need replacement?
8   Has Target received any grant? Is this liable to repayment? Can it be forfeited?
9   Any expenses borne by Target other than for the benefit of Target?

Property

1   Schedule of properties.
2   Purchaser to investigate title or Vendor's solicitors to issue certificate of title?
3   Copies of all deeds and other documents necessary to prove good title.

4   Copies of all insurance policies.
5   Details of any mortgages, charges, leases, tenancies, options, licences, restrictive covenants, easements or other restrictions or rights affecting the properties.
6   Details of all property outgoings.
7   Details of any disputes with adjoining owners (actual or pending).
8   Surveyors' reports?
9   Planning/use restrictions?
10 Necessary planning permissions/ building regulation approvals obtained?
11 Special risks (e.g. mines, flooding, subsidence, landfill, common land, asbestos, deleterious materials, etc.)
12 Any contingent liabilities under previously assigned leases?

Environmental

1   What (if any) environmental due diligence is necessary given nature of business?
2   How does the Target deal with waste, discharge, emission, spillage etc.?
3   Are any environmental licences/consents necessary to conduct business? If so, have they been obtained?
4   Details of any environmental or health and safety disputes with relevant authorities, third parties, or employees.

Employment and Pensions

1   Copies of all standard terms and conditions of employment and details of material deviations.
2   Identify key employees. What is their likely response to the sale? What would be their value to the Target post-acquisition?
3   Details of all directors' service agreements (in particular salaries, notice periods, restrictive covenants and "parachute" provisions).

4 Details of any bonus/profit sharing/option schemes for directors/employees.
5 Identify all existing and potential employee claims against Target.
6 Details of all pension schemes (including actuarial valuations). What are employer's obligations?

Intellectual Property Rights (IPRs)

1 Identify all registered IPRs and conduct necessary searches (i.e. Trade Marks Registry, Patents Office).
2 Identify all material unregistered IPRs.
3 Particulars of any licence agreement granted by or to a third party.
4 Details of any IPR-related disputes (actual or prospective).
5 Particulars of all confidentiality agreements to which the Target is party.
6 Does Target trade under any name other than its full corporate name? Is it protected?

Information Technology

1 Is the processing of any of Target's data under the control of any third party?
2 Do Target's computer systems have adequate capacity for the foreseeable future?
3 What disaster recovery plans are in place?
4 Is any third party software subject to appropriate escrow arrangements?
5 Has Target suffered any material breakdowns in respect of its computer systems?
6 Does Target have adequate backup, security and anti-virus protection?
7 Is Target properly licensed to use the software it actually uses?
8 Is any of Target's software subject to a "time stamp" or "logic bomb" or to the "millennium meltdown".

Taxation

1 Details for the last six years of:
   (a) all Target/Target group tax returns and any prior year still open;
   (b) any agreements with, elections to, clearances from the authorities (obtained or pending).
2 Any intra-group transfer of capital assets in last six years.
3 Any tax liabilities incurred since date of last audited accounts other than in the ordinary course of trading.

Miscellaneous

1 Any other relevant insurance arrangements (product liability/ recall etc.).
2 Any current claims under insurance policies? Are any policies liable to be avoided?
3 Particulars of any other existing or threatened litigation or claims.
4 Compliance with legal obligations.
5 Contingent liabilities (e.g. product liability, guarantees, maintenance obligations, product returns, liabilities under customer incentives etc.).
6 Overseas subsidiaries: What overseas advice is required? What governmental or tax consents are required?

Supplied by Theodore Goddard

8
Approaches to Valuation for Acquisition

Overpaying for an acquisition usually results in failure to achieve the objectives set out at the time of the transaction. Worse, it can seriously damage the acquirer, and in extreme cases can lead to the actual demise of the acquirer. For example, Evode overpaid for Chamberlain Phipps and was later taken over by Laporte. Sony overpaid for CBS, the first in a series of ill-conceived Japanese investments in Hollywood. Sony discovered that there was little logic to the deal, and was faced with a near-insoluble culture clash. On a smaller scale, specialist printing equipment maker Domino took nearly ten years to recover from its disastrous acquisition-led US market entry.

All prospective acquirers must answer two valuation questions:

- How much is the company worth to us?
- What price will be needed to persuade the existing owners to sell to us rather than to someone else, or not at all?

There is no such thing as the correct valuation of a private business or the subsidiary of a group. In practical terms, the valuation is the amount that a purchaser is willing to pay for the business. This can vary enormously: the evidence shows that when at least four provisional written offers are made for a business, the highest one is likely to be at least 50% more than the lowest offer. Occasionally it can be more than double.

VALUATION ISSUES

Rigorous financial analysis is the foundation for valuing a business, but there are less tangible factors that both buyers and sellers should take into account.

Although businesses are bought for their future prospects, history should not be ignored. Consistent and steady growth is preferable to erratic profits and losses during the last three years. Experienced acquirers are often presented with the "hockey stick" projection, by optimistic vendors whose businesses have underperformed but who now predict strong profit growth. Historical numbers should be re-stated to adjust for the effects of one-off events. Purchasers should also recalculate the results for the previous year to show how the business would have performed, using their own accounting policies.

Purchasers buy businesses to benefit from "synergy" as well as the existing profit stream of the business. Experienced acquirers are only too aware that synergy is easier to speculate about than it is to unlock after the acquisition. It is essential to identify precisely how each hoped-for synergy will be unlocked and to calculate its effect in detail before formulating the offer. Chapter 6 describes this process in greater detail. Synergies should be valued, but their value should not be handed over to the seller.

Typically, some 90% of the time spent in valuing a business is spent in researching that business, its competitors, the markets in which it operates and investor confidence in that particular industry at the date of valuation. Weaknesses in valuations, often exposed at the negotiation stage, most often result from a lack of detailed research.

VALUATION TECHNIQUES

Rigorous calculations and projections of adjusted profits and cash flows, together with the current net asset value of the business at the time of completion, are the foundation for any valuation.

The valuation techniques and criteria most commonly used by acquirers and professional advisers are:

- discounted cash flow analysis
- return on investment
- price/earnings ratios
- net asset backing.

Any business valuation should be based on the use of at least two valuation techniques, because any one method tends to have in-built bias.

It must also be remembered that no valuation technique can enhance the inherent accuracy (or rectify the lack of accuracy) in the profit, cash flow and asset value statements. Equally, in a competitive market it would be entirely wrong to assume that an accurate valuation can be made simply by the application of valuation techniques, formulae and criteria. Much less quantifiable factors will be taken into account by competing acquirers which reflect their individual circumstances. These can have a significant impact on the realisable value of a business.

Techniques used in practice are shown by a 1996 survey conducted by Livingstone Guarantee plc, an independent corporate finance house. It reveals the extent to which each of these techniques is applied by acquirers. The survey covered 39 private companies and 35 listed groups. Each was asked which techniques it commonly applied when making acquisitions. The results are set out in Table 8.1.

The results show that acquirers, and especially listed groups, are becoming more sophisticated in their choice of valuation techniques. At least two of the techniques were used by 68% of respondents.

Table 8.1 Use of valuation techniques.

Valuation technique	Listed groups	Private companies
DCF analysis	57%	23%
Return on investment	46%	64%
Price/earning ratios	46%	51%
Net asset backing	15%	59%

Source: Livingstone Guarantee plc

CASH FLOW

Under the cash flow approach the value of the target is the sum of the discounted, after-tax, net cash flows expected following the acquisition, including a terminal value at the end of the analysis period.

The analysis of the cash flow includes the changes which occur as a result of the acquisition:

operating profit	(+)
change in working capital	(±)
depreciation	(+)
capital expenditure	(−)
tax payments	(−)
value of the acquired business at the end of the analysis period	(+)

The net present value of the cash flow is the maximum value of the acquisition to the acquirer. The discount rate should be the acquirer's required post-tax rate of return for businesses in the same risk class as the target.

The main advantage of the cash flow approach is that, unlike the other approaches, it encourages the explicit estimation of:

- changes in future profitability,whether these follow from efficiency improvements consequent on the acquisition, market changes or other sources
- individual profit streams which may have very different characteristics
- changes in the tax circumstances of the business and the timing of tax payments
- any additional capital expenditure that may be required to improve the business or to develop new products in order to sustain the cash flow
- reductions in capital expenditure that might be achieved by better control or focusing of efforts, or sales of peripheral parts of the business
- changes in working capital reflecting turnover growth (increase) or improved financial management (decrease)
- other synergies arising from the acquisition.

Spreadsheets and computer models allow acquirers to carry out sensitivity analyses quickly and accurately to assess the impact of changes in assumptions and policies. The use of such models also helps to make all assumptions explicit, including the benefits expected from the acquisition. Although acquirers should not plan to pay for synergy, they should analyse the difference between the value of the business as it stands and the higher value it might have as part of their group.

RETURN ON INVESTMENT

Return on investment (ROI) provides a good safe target on which a valuation can be based. The downsides of the ROI approach are that it does not demonstrate the cash implications of the deal and that it can be too broad-brush.

The ROI approach to evaluating an acquisition is no different from the standard technique that would be used to appraise any other form of investment. This gives the advantage of allowing simple comparisons between acquisition and alternative business development routes such as start-up.

ROI is calculated by taking adjusted profit before tax in the second full year and dividing it by the total investment; excluding interest charges on the capital. Many listed groups will seek to achieve 25% ROI in the second full year of the investment.

EARNINGS

The most widely used earnings approach to valuing private companies and divisions that do not have market prices of their own is based on the price:earnings (P/E) ratio. An appropriate P/E is determined and applied to an estimate of the sustainable earnings of the target. Care must be taken to ensure that all earnings data is consistently either pre- or post-tax so that like is compared with like. Any multiple applied to pre-tax profit should not be described as a P/E multiple but should be called a pre-tax multiple; it will have a lower than equivalent P/E ratio.

The sustainable earnings to which the P/E ratio is applied should generally exclude exceptional items, interest on investments and cash balances not used in the business, but should include any benefits which can realistically be expected to result from synergy with the acquirer.

The P/E ratio applied to an unquoted target is derived from the P/E ratios of comparable quoted companies. Sector averages are available, but it is not always easy to find genuinely comparable companies in the quoted sector or information on the sale of any comparable private companies. Private companies typically have lower P/E ratios than quoted groups, reflecting the limited liquidity in their shares and the greater risk involved in acquiring private business.

Theoretically the main factors determining a company's P/E ratio are its growth prospects and risk. The better the growth prospects, then in theory the higher the P/E. On the other hand, the greater the risk the lower the P/E, other things being equal.

In practice, however, there is no consistent correlation between current earnings growth and share prices, or between risk and P/E ratios. The earnings figures of individual companies (and hence their P/Es) reflect their gearing and tax positions, and also their accounting policies. These discrepancies may be exacerbated in a period of inflation when earnings figures calculated on an historic cost basis will not be comparable. All these problems mean that the determination of appropriate P/E ratios can be a complex task requiring many judgements and adjustments.

Figure 8.1 maps the trend in P/E ratios paid for private and quoted companies in the UK.

Judiciously applied, the P/E method can provide a useful valuation. Given the subjective nature of the decisions involved, however, P/E valuations can be made to justify whatever the person preparing them wants. The cash flow approach suffers less from this problem as it makes assumptions and estimates more explicitly.

ASSETS

Net assets is a commonly used basis for valuing small private companies, but it has serious drawbacks. The method is mostly reserved for valuing loss-makers or companies operating at

Figure 8.1 *Relative P/E ratios for private and quoted company sales (Source:* BDO Stoy Hayward, *Acquisitions Monthly).*

break-even. The valuation of assets in a company's accounts is rarely useful in the context of an acquisition as:

- historical cost figures are inadequate and current cost figures which might (in theory at least) be preferable are unlikely to be available
- many significant assets may not be valued at all in the accounts – e.g. patents, designs, trade marks, brand names, copyrights, employees, customer lists and contracts
- other assets (such as stock) are frequently overvalued in the accounts. For example, a number of marginally profitable textile companies were sold at a 50% discount to assets in the early 1990s.

Because of these drawbacks, businesses with reasonable performance are likely to change hands at figures substantially higher than their book asset values, the difference between the purchase price and the asset values being called "goodwill". Some businesses require very little by way of assets, and goodwill will be a substantial proportion of the purchase price. By way of contrast, receivers commonly seek prices for businesses which represent a hefty discount on the net asset value.

Thus a purchaser's valuation based on the target's assets needs two elements – a valuation of the assets and an estimation of the goodwill in the business.

As far as the first element goes, expert valuations of land and buildings, stock and plant may be required and other balance sheet items may need careful investigation. The value of work in progress, finished goods and debtors and the adequacy of any provisions need to be assessed. The extent of liabilities to third parties such as overdrafts, other loans and factored debts all need to be accurately determined, as does the company's likely tax liability.

Acquirers are increasingly reluctant to pay substantial sums for unquantifiable goodwill, particularly given recent changes to the UK's accounting regulations and the difficulty of depreciating goodwill. However, many businesses possess few assets and inevitably trade substantially on goodwill. Thus Pearson paid a P/E of over 100 for Software Tool Works, a multimedia developer.

The consideration of how to attach a value to goodwill in a business leads on to the other methods of valuation.

THE METHODS COMPARED

Table 8.2 compares the various valuation methods by setting out their main strengths and weaknesses.

SECTOR-SPECIFIC BENCHMARKS

In addition to the standard valuation methods set out above it is also useful to apply any sector-specific benchmarks that may

Table 8.2   *Comparison of valuation methods.*

	Strengths	Weaknesses
P/E ratios	Based on market rate	Does not take account of cash effect
DCF	Reflects view on future cash flow	Difficult to calculate in practice
ROI	Good, safe target comparable to other investment projects	Does not take account of cash effect; broad brush
Net asset backing	Provides a comfort factor in worst case	May not reflect benefit to buyer

Table 8.3 *Sector-specific valuation benchmarks.*

Industry/business	Valuation benchmark
Landfill	Price per cubic metre
Advertising agencies	Multiple of billings
Mobile telephone service	Price per subscriber
Cable TV	Price per subscriber
Fund managers	Multiple of funds under management
Hotels	Sale price per room
Mining companies	Value of mineral reserves
Professional firms	Multiple of fee income
Petrol retailers	Multiple of annual gallonage
Ready mixed concrete	Price per cubic metre of output

exist. These are not a substitute for valuation but can be a very valuable guideline. Examples of sector-specific benchmarks are set out in Table 8.3.

COMBINING THE METHODS

It is a good idea to make estimates using at least two of the above methods and to seek to understand any differences between the results. The differences typically reflect the weaknesses of each method, subject always to the underlying assumptions being consistent and reasonable. For example, businesses that require few physical assets (such as products with a high service and support element) will obviously have a low asset value. In this case, the high values arrived at based on the P/E or cash flow approaches may be more reasonable.

The cash flow approach can explicitly take account of factors ignored in a P/E calculation. One such factor might be the capital expenditure needed to bring the facilities in a small business up to the health and safety standards required by a large acquirer. Such investment would make the cash flow valuation lower than a straightforward P/E figure.

Another common reason for divergence between P/E and cash

flow valuations results from the selection of P/E ratios and discount rates that are inconsistent.

Whatever method of valuation is adopted, the maximum the acquirer should pay for the business is the valuation less the present value of its liabilities.

VALUE TO THE SELLER

The buyer needs to estimate the minimum amount the owners will accept, taking account of all known factors. The methods available to estimate the value of the target to existing owners are of course the same as those outlined above for buyers. Clearly, however, they should take no account of the benefits of synergy or improvements resulting from the acquisition.

Special circumstances may influence the value to the owners of continuing in business. For instance, one or more of the shareholders may wish to retire, or the business may have short-term liquidity problems which can reduce the price at which the owners would sell. The existence of other interested buyers, though, will exert an upward influence on price. In the special case of a business in receivership, the creditors' alternative (in the absence of other buyers) is to break up the business and sell the assets at auction.

Sellers can benefit from scarcity value if they own a business in a market that is short of available acquisition targets. Some sellers fail to recognise, however, that scarcity value is often temporary. Frustrated acquirers will sometimes respond by entering the market through start-up or by acquiring a much smaller player and investing for its growth. The over-ambitious seller is then faced with fewer prospective purchasers and increased competition as well, reducing the benefit of the original scarcity value.

Buyers should keep in mind that apart from other competing buyers the sector may have various alternatives to a trade sale. Most sellers will at least consider the alternatives of sale to the management team or a financial purchaser, or flotation on the stock market.

For quoted companies, the market price offers a guide to the likely sale price, although a premium is normally required to persuade existing owners to sell. The premium is driven partly by the bidder's need to buy the target's shares over a short period of time. The problem is to assess the extent to which the market price at the time of the bid already reflects bid speculation. Bid premiums can be 20–50% of the market price three months or so before the bid, but they vary widely from case to case.

Unquoted companies are generally valued at a discount relative to their quoted counterparts. The discount, usually between 30% and 60% reflects the inferior marketability of unquoted shares.

CONCLUSION

Quoted or unquoted, the soundest method for valuing acquisition targets is cash flow. It leaves out fewer important aspects than other methods and quantifies more assumptions. It is less subject to manipulation to produce a result in support of unsound thinking by company strategists.

It is important to remember that:

- the value of a business is what one or more purchasers are prepared to pay for it
- successful deals, particularly including the complexities of an earn-out, are only struck between reasonable people acting reasonably.

CASE STUDY 7: VALUATION OF WIDGETCO FOR BUYCO

Widgetco is a well established private manufacturing business owned by a husband and wife team. They wish to retire from the business and, with the help of professional advisers, have obtained an offer from an acquisitive quoted group, called Buyco.

Widgetco has always been cash positive and, despite occasional "hiccups", the owners have neither felt they needed strict financial control nor appointed a qualified accountant to produce the management accounts. They rely on a quarterly visit from Widgetco's auditors to produce management information. Being a private company, the owners pay themselves well.

Widgetco dominates a niche in its engineering marketplace and exports a significant proportion of its sales. The husband, although MD, concentrates on the sales and marketing role, and his wife is administrative director. Widgetco also has a first-class production director and a sales and marketing director, both of whom were recruited from major organisations about three years ago, as the owners then recognised the need to strengthen the management team as the company grew. The four senior managers prepare an annual budget together in the autumn of each year for the next financial year.

Widgetco's recent financial performance, as shown in its audited accounts, is summarised below:

Summary profit and loss accounts (£000)
Year ended 31 December

	1993 Actual audited	1994 Actual audited	1995 Actual audited	9 months ended 30 September 1996 Actual management
Sales	4210	5050	5986	5063
Gross margin	1347	1566	1975	1671
Other costs	1310	1505	1818	1680
Profit/(loss) before interest and tax	37	61	157	(9)
Interest receivable	13	7	14	4
Pre-tax profit/(loss)	50	68	171	(5)

Buyco wishes to pay cash for 100% of Widgetco's shares, with the owners staying on only for a six-month handover period. The sales and marketing director is managing director designate and, with the owners' full agreement, Buyco intends to appoint a qualified accountant as financial controller.

Based on information provided by Widgetco's auditors, Buyco has reconstructed Widgetco's P&L and included the recently produced budget to show the "sustainable" levels of profits set out below. The business is not materially seasonal and Buyco believes it reasonable to extrapolate a full year forecast from the September 1996 management accounts, particularly as order intake has been slightly above budget in October and sales through to 31 December are now relatively predictable.

Profit and loss

	1993 Actual	1994 Actual	1995 Actual	1996 Forecast	1997 Budget
Sales	4210	5050	5986	6750	7700
Gross margin	1347	1566	1975	2230	2540
Other costs	(1310)	(1505)	(1818)	(2105)	(2236)
Add back:					
"Excess directors" remuneration	91	103	85	137	–
One-off bad debt	–	65	–	–	–
Sustainable profit before interest and tax	128	229	242	262	304
Interest receivable	13	7	14	6	12
Sustainable pre-tax profit	141	236	256	268	316

Directors' remuneration	1993 Actual	1994 Actual	1995 Actual	1996 Actual
MD– actual	138	154	150	182
– market rate	(60)	(65)	(70)	(75)
Excess	78	89	80	107
Administrative director – actual	43	48	42	70
Financial controller – market rate	(30)	(34)	(37)	(40)
Excess	13	14	5	30
Total excess	91	103	85	137

Outline Valuation

Return on Investment (ROI)

Buyco anticipates that all available synergies from the acquisition will have been generated relatively soon, by 31 December 1997. Buyco requires a 20% return on its total investment in Widgetco by the end of 1997. Widgetco will generate the cash needed for all its capital expenditure until then and Buyco's professional costs will be in the region of £75 000 to complete the acquisition.

Therefore using ROI the maximum price Buyco should pay is:

$$\text{Price} = \frac{£304\,000}{20\%} - £75\,000$$

$$= £1\,445\,000$$

Price: Earnings Ratio

By analysing the P/Es of similar and related quoted companies (and then applying an appropriate discount), and also looking at the multiples paid in recent similar deals, Buyco arrives at a comparative P/E to apply in this instance of 9.0. This is comfortably lower than its own P/E of 17.3.

Therefore, based upon Widgetco's latest audited results in 1995, the most Buyco should pay is:

$$\text{Price} = (£256\,000 - 33\% \text{ corporation tax}) \times 9.0$$

$$= £172\,000 \times 9.0$$

$$= £1\,548\,000$$

Net Asset Value (NAV)

At 30 September, Widgetco had a NAV of £956 000. It is inappropriate to rely solely on NAV to calculate the value of a business unless it is loss making. In the case of Widgetco taking the ROI and P/E bases of valuation into account, a goodwill premium of about £0.5 million is appropriate.

Because Widgetco is not able to produce financial projections for at least five years, it was not possible for Buyco to carry out a discounted cash flow (DCF) valuation.

Conclusion

Buyco concluded that it would be prepared to pay up to £1.5

million in cash for Widgetco, provided the business made at least £268 000 of sustainable pre-tax profits in the year ended 31 December 1996; and had a NAV at that date of at least £1.0 million.

Supplied by Livingstone Guarantee for this publication

9
Negotiation and Deal Structuring

Much has been published elsewhere on this subject. This section presents an overview of the key issues.

Checklist 4 sets out some guidelines for negotiation.

Many of the guidelines given in Checklist 4 are common sense: a negotiation to buy a company is similar to many other negotiations, although the complexity of an acquisition and the size of the stakes naturally create difficulties. Experienced negotiators emphasise that careful project management and creating an atmosphere of consensus are the two most important steps for success.

Negotiations can break down for a multitude of reasons. The acquisition of Courtauld's woollens business by Drummond was concluded only because a third party managed to bring the parties together again after they had fallen out over an inconsequential detail. It is common for negotiations to start up again after some difficulties have slowed the process. Potential acquirers should never burn their bridges.

WALK-AWAY PRICE

The golden rule for all acquirers is not to overpay. As emphasised in Chapter 8 and as shown by the AMR/ICME acquisition survey, the single greatest reason for the failure of acquisitions is that the buyers paid too much. To contain the enthusiasm of

---

CHECKLIST 4

Negotiating guidelines

For the Overall Process

- Request an exclusivity agreement.
- Set out a realistic timetable; ensure it suits both sides.
- Agree the approach up front; agree a mechanism for making any necessary changes to it.
- Allocate specific responsibilities to members of both teams.
- Avoid confusion over what has been agreed – write it down.
- If possible, nominate someone to run the negotiations (this could be an adviser).
- Hold the negotiations in appropriate venues, taking account of whose "territory" they are on.

For the Acquirer in Particular

- Win the trust and confidence of the seller's shareholders and management.
- Do not alienate any key individuals.
- Spot sensitivities in advance; handle each one with care.
- Do not pretend that the seller's unresolved key concerns have gone away if they have not been mentioned for some time.
- Speak to the sellers in their own language and in a way that does not antagonise them.
- Use all the information you have to your benefit.
- Consider carefully the timing of any key moves and suggestions.
- Do not allow personal agendas or emotion to take over.
- If necessary use outsiders and advisers to take the blame at tricky times (e.g. misunderstandings on price).

---

management who have set their hearts on completing a deal (at any price), a walk-away price should be set. This is the price beyond which the acquirer is not prepared to go as the price will no longer be justified by the valuation.

Every acquirer should enter negotiations with a clear view of the walk-away price. A company chairperson will usually insist that any premium has to be quantified in detail. A common question they ask is, "Would you put your own money into it?", which serves to focus the mind admirably.

As discussed in Chapter 8, the right price to pay for a business depends on the nature and quality of its activities and other key considerations such as tax. It also depends on the situation of the acquirer, which means that the "right price" will be different for different acquirers.

PRIVATE SALE

When negotiating the acquisition of a private or management-owned business with a range of shareholders such as an owner-manager, other directors and staff, venture capitalists or passive family shareholders, it is essential to satisfy the often diverse requirements of each shareholder group. For example, the owner-manager who is retained to run the business may be delighted to accept much of the consideration in shares and a seat on the Group board; the venture capital firm is far more likely to demand cash as the realisation of its investment. The first necessary steps are to understand the "zone of potential agreement" with each set of shareholders and to determine the balance of power between the sellers in terms of both voting rights and persuasiveness.

If owner-managers are to be retained, it is essential that the deal will motivate the sellers correctly after the transaction has been completed. Solid financial incentives and fulfilling roles will be far more motivating than a supposedly water-tight service contract. However, maintaining the attention and motivation of a former owner-manager after acquisition is very difficult. With cash in the bank and a new set of rules to abide by, many soon become frustrated and leave.

One solution that is often attempted is to provide the former owner-manager with a "larger" role in the organisation. This solution fails depressingly often: David Lloyd's walk-out from Whitbread 12 months after making £20 million from the sale of his leisure centre business is a typical example.

Even when the owner-manager does not leave, giving him or

her a larger role may mean playing to their weaknesses instead of their strengths: they lose their focus on running the business they know well and get involved in things they may not be good at.

In the case of private company transactions all these considerations must be well planned if they are not to lead to significant difficulties.

EARN-OUTS

An earn-out is an agreement that a vendor party earns part of his or her consideration for the sale of the business at a specified time after the deal is struck, and in proportion to the acquired business' performance measured against predetermined targets. Earn-outs fell from favour after their extensive use in the 1980s, as they often led to disputes. In many cases, however, they remain appropriate, especially where there is a low net asset backing compared to the overall valuation, and where there are particular risks concerning key owner managers, customers or suppliers. Although some acquirers are now strongly prejudiced against earn-out deals, an earn-out is sometimes the only way to bridge the gap between a vendor's price requirements and an acquirer's view of acceptable deal value and risk.

Obviously, the rationale of earn-outs is to motivate vendors who remain as managers to boost profitability. Badly structured earn-out deals can result in the opposite, as they can incentivise managers to reduce investment in the business to a minimum. Sensible investment targets need to be set from the outset. For businesses where growth can reasonably be forecast, one solution can be to propose a final price based on the average of sales and a multiple of earnings. Basing a valuation on a multiple of sales alone is highly dangerous.

Earn-outs have the attraction of making sellers prove their promises of future sustained profitability. They can be highly contentious to implement and should be avoided as a quick fix to any negotiating difficulty or falling out over price. For an earn-out to stand a chance of working it is essential that there is empathy between buyer and seller. It is very rare that a later cold interpretation of the earn-out terms are exactly in line with the original intentions of the parties. Both parties should beware if either side acts aggressively to maximise its own benefit – the resulting dispute can be bitter, and can have unforeseen consequences in court.

Situations when an earn-out deal may be essential to reach a mutually acceptable deal include:

- where asset backing is low compared to the business value. In service companies the net tangible assets may be 20% or less of the total business valuation
- where the business is particularly dependent on one customer or client. A successful PR consultancy business relied on one client for 35% of its total revenue. The vendors' view that they had an excellent relationship with this major client was regarded by the prospective purchaser as nothing more than a statement of faith
- where the business is particularly dependent on one or two key owner managers.

Earn-outs are typically a feature of acquisitions of private companies. They are rare in acquisitions of a subsidiary or division of a group.

As mentioned above, it is usually sensible to base an earn-out on profit targets. In order to avoid disagreement and litigation, it is essential to define carefully what is meant by profit.

Generally, it should be profit before tax because tax planning should be handled at group level. The definition of profit should specify:

- The accounting policies to be used.
- The cost of any services to be provided to the business by the purchaser and how these will be calculated. Sellers will often claim that "management charges" levied by the acquirer do not correspond to any real benefit and therefore should be disregarded when calculating earn-out profit.
- Where finance is provided by the group, the interest rate that will be charged. It is unreasonable for sellers to expect "free" finance during the earn-out period.

Earn-outs of course can be based on a financial measures other than profit. Commission income was used in the case of a retail travel agency chain, where the acquirer wished to make changes throughout the cost structure of the business but where the continued activity of the owner-manager was important in a marketing role.

It is reasonable for the sellers to ask to provide the managing director throughout the earn-out period. This person along with any other continuing owner-managers may well expect to receive service contracts for the duration of the earn-out period to ensure that they cannot be dismissed prematurely, because this would impair their ability to maximise the deferred consideration. Better still, the service contracts should extend to about four months after the end of the earn-out period so that the shareholder directors are still employed while final accounts are being prepared and agreed.

It is generally inadvisable to have an earn-out period of longer than two years from the beginning of the acquirer's next financial year. An earn-out period of three years should generally be regarded as a maximum. The purpose of an earn-out is usually to ensure the commitment of the previous owners to achieving continued profit growth during the critical period after the change of ownership, and in most cases two years is sufficient.

SALE OF A SUBSIDIARY

The deal structuring required for the sale of a subsidiary can be more straightforward. The vendor will rarely be interested in the shares of the purchaser. Some forms of delayed consideration can be considered, however. The simplest form is where the buyer agrees to buy an initial stake in the business, with an option to increase its shareholding to 100% if certain targets are achieved.

Sometimes acquirers agree to buy a company outright, but stripped of its debts and tax liabilities. These extra costs are added to the consideration at a later stage if certain performance targets are achieved.

BUYING ASSETS OR BUYING EQUITY

There are two ways of buying a business:

- buying assets – the acquisition of tangible assets used good-will, and the assumption of certain specified liabilities
- buying equity – the acquisition of shares in a company carrying on the business.

The decision between the two methods depends on a number of factors and will be the subject of negotiation to balance the conflicting interests of the buyer and the seller. For example, where the price represents a premium over book value, the seller may prefer a share sale whereas the buyer may prefer an assets sale.

Buyers will often favour asset sales as in theory it enables them to select those assets and liabilities they are prepared to take over. A further advantage to the buyer is that immediate tax relief may be available on the purchase of assets.

TAX

Tax structuring can be a deal-maker and a deal-breaker. Expert tax advice can close the gap between the aspirations of sellers, private or public, and a purchaser's valuation. Tax issues are covered in great detail in other places, and are beyond the scope of this guide.

CONCLUSION

- Negotiating is not just about being tough: a skilled negotiator will plan and manage the process to suit a personal agenda while taking care not to alienate the other side.
- Deal structuring can be critical; it requires a clear understanding of both parties' requirements, plus the skills and the imagination to find ways of bridging the gap between them.

10
Using the Law to Protect the Buyer

INTRODUCTION

The best acquisition contract is the one that neither party has cause to refer to, and which stays firmly in the bottom draw.

The potential acquirer's lawyers' brief can be split into three main areas:

- spotting problems that are yet to arise and solving them in advance of the deal being signed
- seeking protection in areas of uncertainty that could impact the value of the business by using warranties and indemnities
- assessing the cost and feasibility of potentially contentious post-acquisition actions.

PROBLEM SPOTTING

Many of the problems, or potential problems, that an investigating lawyer should spot are not necessarily caused by an intention to deceive. Many are not caused by incompetence either. It can simply be that no one spotted the potentially negative implications of specific actions in the long term, or in the event of a change of ownership.

For example, if a technology business is created by two partners, and then becomes a limited liability company at a later stage in its development, the founders may not realise the need to transfer the intellectual property to the new entity. The business can trade satisfactorily with the intellectual property vested in the founders. However, if the company is subsequently acquired, the new owner must be prepared for the eventual departure of one of the founders.

A change of ownership can lead to undesirable contractual changes in what was otherwise a satisfactory situation. Contracts with suppliers or partners operating under licence agreements can adversely be affected by an acquisition. For example, a deal could be halted by a change of ownership clause buried in an agreement between a distribution company and a major supplier with whom negotiations have been difficult over the preceding years.

Once problems of these types have been identified they can, in the majority of cases, be raised and solved. They will often give rise to the need to negotiate with suppliers or employees. Alternatively, warranties and indemnities can be used for protection. The process of problem spotting and the subsequent negotiations can often add to the time required to complete a deal, and to the cost of legal advice.

WARRANTIES AND INDEMNITIES

If statements made by the seller turn out to have been incorrect when they were given (in other words, if they are misrepresentations), they may entitle a buyer to damages. It may also be possible to set aside the contract.

Warranties and indemnities are an increasingly important aspect of any acquisition agreement. In the 1960s and 1970s, few were attached to any agreement; they can now form a substantial part of the agreement, and of the preceding negotiation. Warranties, representations and indemnities in the acquisition agreement are designed to limit the dangers encapsulated in the phrase *caveat emptor* – buyer beware.

Warranties and indemnities seek to provide protection in different ways. A **warranty** is a guarantee that a particular set of circumstances is as set out. If this guarantee turns out not to be the case and if it affects the value of the target business, the purchaser is entitled to what is effectively a discount on the price paid for the business. An **indemnity** is a guaranteed, specified financial remedy. If the indemnity is triggered, the benefit is payable regardless of whether or not the value of the acquired company is affected by the failure to comply. The benefit is generally one pound for every pound of damage, subject to the financial standing of the seller.

Although the principle of *caveat emptor* applies to the acquisition of all businesses, it is unusual for listed companies to be required to provide extensive warranties and indemnities. Acquirers of unlisted companies, on the other hand, almost always require sellers to provide wide-ranging guarantees and indemnities, as a method of reducing risk.

How the Two Sides See Warranties and Indemnities

Purchasers use warranties to obtain compensation if the reality of the purchase does not correspond with what they thought they were buying. Sellers, on the other hand, will always prefer the principle *caveat emptor* and will seek to conclude the sale with the minimum number of warranties and indemnities, giving rise to as few potential liabilities as possible.

From the purchaser's point of view the key questions are:

- What warranties and indemnities are required?
- What is the procedure to establish breach?
- What is the procedure to claim damages for breach?
- Are the damages recoverable by other means higher?
- In limited cases, might there be a right to rescind the contract?
- Can restrictive time limits be avoided if these are applied to claims under the warranties?
- Can a cap on liability be avoided?

The seller will be keen to:

- get the terms of the disclosure letter right
- restrict when and how any form of claim can be made
- put in place a maximum overall claim level and a limit on any individual claim
- attempt to restrict or exclude other forms of claim beyond those set out.

Indemnities

An indemnity is a guaranteed solution against a specific liability. The most common indemnity is against tax liabilities. This is a promise by the seller to meet a particular liability should it arise. In this case it makes sense for it to be measured pound for pound, as opposed to representing a reduction in the value of the acquisition. Another case where indemnities are used is the performance of specific non-recurring contracts.

Indemnities are generally of a more limited nature than warranties. However, many of the issues relevant to indemnity claims are the same as for warranties.

Nature and Scope of Warranties

During the course of negotiations, a seller and the seller's advisers may make many statements about the company. Some may be statements of fact on which the purchaser bases the decision to buy or the valuation. The purchaser should ensure that any key statements about which there exists some doubt are used as the basis of warranties.

Warranties are designed to:

- provide the purchaser with as much protection as possible
- force the vendor to be thorough and accurate in statements made in the discovery (or disclosure) letter.

Warranties are contractual terms. If these terms are breached the buyer can claim for damages. The new owner of a business will have to show three things if the purchase does not match expectations, namely:

- there was a breach of a specific warranty
- that this was not excluded by being disclosed in the discovery letter
- that the breach has resulted in a specific reduction in the value of the company, compared to the price paid.

As it is the disclosure letter which limits the scope of the warranties, the seller will use this as well as the terms of the agreement to avoid risk.

The Disclosure Letter

The disclosure letter is a vital document as it provides much of the information on which the buyer bases a decision. Lawyers argue over whether or not the disclosure letter is a contractual document; it can be incorporated into the contract by reference. However, for all practical purposes it does not really matter so long as the acquisition agreement expressly refers to its effect.

The real debate is over the terms of the disclosure letter. If the disclosure letter deals with an issue accurately and specifically, there is no claim to be had over that issue. In the disclosure letter it is facts that must be disclosed and not the consequences of those facts. However, it is not enough for the seller to have mentioned certain facts which, if properly investigated, might have allowed the purchaser to discover the problem. For example, a simple statement that a site was formerly used for electroplating is insufficient if an environmental liability is knowingly being incurred.

Claims

A claim for misrepresentation can arise from statements made:

- in the pre-contractual negotiations
- during due diligence
- in the acquisition agreement itself
- in the documents disclosed with the disclosure letter.

The vendor has little control over statements made by employees during due diligence, and thus will make every effort to avoid liability. The vendor may seek to do this by including an "entire agreement clause", or an exclusion clause, or possibly both. An entire agreement clause states that the purchaser has not relied on any representation or undertaking whether oral or in writing except those that are expressly incorporated in the agreement.

The astute buyer will use a combination of common sense and further investigation during due diligence to check out those statements made by employees which appear doubtful. It is a mistake to rely too heavily on warranties and to attempt to reduce the need for diligent investigation by bundling as many potential problem areas as possible under warranties: there is no guarantee that claims will be accepted, or if they are, that the cost of pursuing them will be worthwhile.

Restrictions on When and How a Claim can be Made

As soon as a breach of warranty is found, the purchaser must consider the restrictions in the acquisition agreement on making a claim. These may be:

- shorter time limits than the statutory six-year period
- formal requirements for giving notice of the claim.

Quantifying the claim can be difficult. A key point for the purchaser is to maintain a consistent position throughout; it should not change its mind between the original notice and the basis for litigation.

Measures of Damages

It should be straightforward to work out how much can be gained from a successful warranty claim. In principle the purchaser is entitled to the difference between the value of the company or business as warranted and its actual market value. The trouble is that in practice this principle is not always easy to apply.

The purchase price is generally taken as the warranted value and one of the standard methods of valuation is applied to assess the company's market value. The problem area is relating the purchase price to the warranted value where a purchaser has paid a premium for private reasons. So, the purchase price will not always reflect the warranted value and any attempt to claim will start from a losing position. Also, there will inevitably be a dispute over the method of valuation which should be used. This can be highly tortuous as there is no such thing as a correct value for a company, let alone a correct valuation method. Each party will argue for the method that produces the most favourable valuation for its purposes.

A further complicating factor is the question of contributory negligence in contractual claims. The seller can argue that the actions of the new owner, who did not understand the business or did not know how to manage it correctly, caused the value of the company to decline.

Restrictions on the Amount Recoverable

The seller will generally impose both a minimum and a maximum level of claim. The ceiling of liability is often fixed at the amount of the consideration paid for the company. Obviously, this would be a matter of negotiation. The scope of these limits can be a further factor which makes the law an unattractive route when seeking to obtain a solution.

The availability of non-contractual remedies should always be considered. It may be advantageous to the purchaser not to rely on contract, and the warranties and indemnities which were hammered out in it, but to find a solution through negotiation.

Conclusion: Warranties and Indemnities

Although an acquirer can seek financial protection from the unexpected by imposing detailed warranties and indemnities, it is not always worth pursuing them. It is not often that claims for breach of warranties or indemnities get as far as the courts, but the costs can still be high and the outcome uncertain. Generally, decisions are made to settle claims at a fairly early stage. Ironically, often a commercially sound settlement requires that the costs of instructing lawyers, obtaining independent reports and interviewing witnesses will probably all be incurred before settlement negotiations even begin.

An acquirer should consider at the outset whether alternative dispute resolution rather than litigation would be in the interests of both sides. An agreement to use mediation or determination by an expert to resolve disputed claims can offer the best solution.

Perhaps the greatest advantage of warranties and indemnities is that they focus the attention of the seller during negotiation. The imposition of warranties causes the seller to get the facts straight; this gives the acquirer confidence of a clear view of key aspects which impact the value of the business.

REVIEWING POTENTIAL POST-ACQUISITION ACTIONS

Before a business is acquired it is essential that the new owner has at least an outline of the plan for integration. It is the implementation of this plan which will lead to the value-added sought by the acquirer. The first two areas of legal involvement are problem spotting within the existing business and seeking protection through warranties and indemnities. The third area of legal work relates to understanding the practicality of proposed post-acquisition actions and assessing their impact on the business.

Depending on the proposed post-acquisition actions, consideration should be given to the following questions:

- What recourse would directors or employees have if their contracts were severed?
- What recourse would they have if their terms and conditions are altered?
- What will the reaction be to aligning the pension schemes?
- Can employees be prevented from leaving and setting up in competition?
- Are there any restrictions on the change of use or closure of sites?

Overall the greatest problems likely to arise are people related. TUPE, The Transfer of Undertakings (Protection of Employment) Regulations, will be widely referred to by any investigating lawyer as they are the major regulations in the area. Legal advice should be taken on the nature, timing and communication of restructuring. In some cases lawyers will advise acquirers to delay certain restructuring actions, as rapid action can lead to an unfavourable outcome under TUPE.

Levels of severance pay will also be highly sensitive. An extreme example of problems encountered on severance is that of John Clark, former head of BET, who sued Rentokil for loss of employment after the BET hostile bid. He sought £5 million and was awarded £3 million.

In the comparatively liberal employment market of the UK these problems can often appear onerous. In continental Europe they can be much more so. In France, for example, a new owner will have to implement a new social plan if the business is to be restructured. United Biscuits, when reversing out of its ill-fated French manufacturing venture in 1996, found the cost of reducing employee numbers in France can be 150% of the equivalent cost in the UK.

WHO TO USE

Lawyers will play a significant role in any acquisition agreement. There are few major differences between the large law firms. An acquirer is best advised to select a partner of a firm, whom he or she trusts and with whom communication is very clear. The best lawyers do not operate by religiously following checklists. A strong sense of problem spotting is essential, as is the ability to negotiate with the buyer in a pragmatic way which can lead to a satisfactory outcome for all sides.

CONCLUSION

Some acquirers advise that lawyers should be brought in late in the process, thus reducing their opportunity to run up large bills. This is good advice, but it is even more important to make sure that the lawyers have the opportunity to do their job properly and to reach a satisfactory agreement for all sides. There should then be every chance that the agreement will stay in the bottom drawer.

11
Management and the Human Factor

DELIVERING THE BENEFITS

However impressive the potential benefits of an acquisition, they have to be delivered if the transaction is to be worthwhile for shareholders. This will almost always require change, and this in turn makes the human factor critical.

When acquisitions are being planned and negotiated, human resource issues tend to take second place to commercial and financial considerations. Indeed, the human factor is often neglected altogether. Yet many acquisitions disappoint, despite promising potential synergies and other business logic, precisely because of the negative effects of the event on the people involved. This observation is backed up by a growing body of research.

A well-known example is Fisons' difficulty in integrating VG Instruments into its scientific division: Fisons' management were unable to blend VG's technically focused research and development groups into their existing distribution-oriented activities. Equally, Thorn never managed to integrate its culture with EMI, despite a series of endless reorganisations.

In service businesses it is commonplace that people are paramount. The same applies in publishing, and countless failed acquisitions there are attributed to culture clashes. For example, the two cultures of Time and Warner remain poles apart and the world's largest media group has been among the least profitable during the 1990s. The problem is compounded in France where the *Clause de Conscience* law protects editorial freedom comprehensively and gives editors the right to leave with attractive packages if their company is acquired.

Sometimes the warning signs of human resource problems emerge soon after the formal announcement of an acquisition. Sometimes they take longer to materialise. They include:

- increased staff turnover
- reduced productivity and overall performance
- projects being delivered late
- low morale.

The wider the cultural gap between the two organisations, the more difficult and challenging the implementation of change and integration.

Figure 11.1, from the AMR/ICME survey, sets out the correlation between closeness of culture and success of integration. That these effects should occur is unsurprising. Change is only successful if it is supported by the people affected by it. Most people dislike change, and they dislike the sort of uncertainty that arises from an acquisition. The more radical the change, the more people will resist it – especially if they think it is being badly handled. On the other hand, people expect change after an acquisition and a failure to act swiftly will result in confusion all round and can seriously damage the investment.

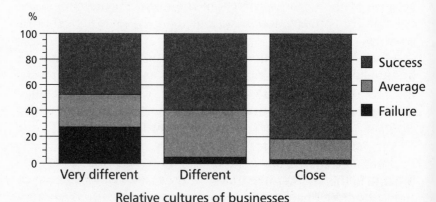

Figure 11.1 *Correlation between closeness of culture and success of integration (Source: AMR/ICME survey).*

It is easy to explain why negative effects may occur. It is harder to say how to prevent them from happening in the first place. Perhaps the most important point is to act swiftly. Successful and experienced acquirers such as Williams Holdings, BTR and Reed Elsevier prepare their post-acquisition management plans before executing an acquisition, and start to implement change within the first few days of taking ownership.

Preparation will help avoid management and staff problems. Organisational and human resource issues should be addressed throughout the whole acquisition process, including:

- acquisition strategy development
- pre-acquisition research and evaluation
- post-acquisition integration.

HUMAN RESOURCE ISSUES DURING ACQUISITION STRATEGY DEVELOPMENT

If the people dimension of an acquisition is to be handled successfully, it has to be considered from the outset. People and cultural issues must be considered when deciding whether combining two businesses makes sense.

A horizontal acquisition that meets specific criteria of fit in terms of products or distribution channels may be highly problematic if it involves two wholly different sets of culture, management style and organisational structure, for instance. Some of the mergers in the late 1980s between High Street building societies failed to result in the development of unified and identifiable corporate cultures, and the new businesses struggled to perform as anticipated. In another example, Staveley, a British engineering group, sought to integrate Mid-West and West Coast businesses in the USA; the culture gap made the task particularly difficult.

Some substantial difficulties have been encountered in deals between UK companies and Central European partners. Case Study 8 in this chapter illustrates the difficulties of these acquisitions. While Central European acquisitions offer the UK partner significant advantages such as low labour costs, the businesses have difficulty performing well in the short term, given the

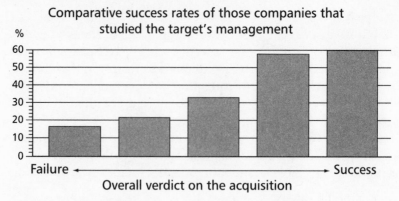

Figure 11.2   *Correlation between successful acquisition and investigating management (Source: AMR/ICME survey).*

Central European enterprises' underinvestment in management, education and product development over many years.

Chapters 6, 7 and 8 show that understanding the potential benefit of an acquisition to shareholders requires more than simple financial evaluation; the most effective risk reducer prior to commitment to an acquisition is commercial due diligence. In drawing up a specification for such research, acquirers are well advised to provide for a profile of the target's human resources, including information on organisational structure, managerial competence and employee relations.

Figure 11.2 taken from the AMR/ICME survey, demonstrates the direct correlation between successful acquisition and investigating management.

HUMAN RESOURCES ISSUES DURING PRE-ACQUISITION RESEARCH

A full-scale investigation of a target's human resources may only be possible after a deal has been struck. The vendor will not always encourage or accept organisational investigations which, by involving key people, may appear obtrusive and disruptive. Nonetheless as management quality will almost always form a central part of the thorough analysis of a target business this area must be covered.

If the vendor refuses access to management, for whatever reason, this can be a legitimate deal-stopper. However, the imaginative acquirer can often find a way around objections to access by proposing a related activity such as joint venture or project discussions. Another approach, with the co-operation of the seller, is to suggest the visit by an independent pensions adviser to review existing or possible pensions policies.

Checklist 5 sets out a list of human resource issues for acquirers to address before taking control of a business.

Even without the co-operation of the vendor, it is possible to gain important insights to management style and any difficulties. During the due diligence process, competitors, customers and distributors can be interviewed to obtain information on the target's management. Former employees are often excellent sources of information, although what they say must be interpreted in the light of the circumstances of their departure. When access is granted to the business during evaluation, a limited programme of sensitively organised management and staff interviews need not raise suspicions or cause undue concern.

Investigating these management and staff issues prior to acquisition allows acquirers to assess the actions with regard to the target's people. It allows acquirers to take a view as to whether the various levels of management in the target company will be positive towards the acquisition and, if so, whether they will be capable of delivering the performance required under the new circumstances.

Moreover, the acquiring company needs to judge whether it has the management resources itself to handle the integration process and, if necessary, to provide continuing support. Those charged with going into the newly acquired business, taking control, and initiating the planned changes may face indifference or hostility. Their behaviour towards managers and staff, and the way they communicate their intentions can be crucial determinants of the acquisition's future. It is risky to trust the selection of those people to judgement alone. Human resource management can play an important role in identifying, possibly with the help of psychometric instruments, the right people to move into the target company.

An acquirer can learn a great deal about the target in the course of the negotiations over the terms of sale. While the negotiating

CHECKLIST 5

Human Resource Investigation Checklist

Management

What is the calibre of key managers?

What is the extent of delegation throughout the organisation?

What are the management values? How are they communicated?

What is the management style? How has it evolved?

Organisation

What formal and informal structures are in place? How do they relate to reporting lines?

What systems are in place? How effective are they and how frequently are they reviewed?

Staff

What is the staff turnover level? How has it varied historically and by business group?

What are the various levels of staff ability? How are they assessed?

What is the involvement and commitment of staff? How much scope is there for improvement?

What is the level of responsiveness to change?

Is there trade union representation? How strong is it?

team is concentrating on the commercial, financial and legal details, a human resources expert can pick up useful information on the target's culture, the values held by its management, and the way people are managed. This information should be fed back to the managers who take responsibility for integrating the two businesses. It can also be used to fine-tune the plans for detailed research and for subsequent integration activities.

It may be, for instance, that the target is structured hierarchically and is heavily reliant on overt control mechanisms, allowing little freedom or autonomy to individuals. The culture of the acquiring company, by contrast, may be innovative and creative, expressed in flat organisational structures with minimal control mechanisms, and expecting its acquisitions to behave innovatively in their own markets. In this case, detailed and specific plans for organisational change will be required.

In "people businesses", such as media or business services, it is essential to assess whether key individuals will stay. Service agreements can reduce the risk of wholesale departures, but they cannot be relied on as perfect solutions. Many entrepreneurs find the shock of conforming to public company reporting standards too much to handle and leave before the full duration of their contracts. There is also the danger of the entrepreneur using the proceeds of the sale to start again. One would-be French media baron started a second business two years after selling out to a British group, and while still contracted to run the business he sold to that acquirer.

HUMAN RESOURCE ISSUES DURING POST-ACQUISITION INTEGRATION

Perhaps the most common mistake made by acquirers is to underestimate the time and effort required to plan and then deliver the integration of an acquisition into their business portfolio. Given the strategic nature of acquisition and the sums potentially at risk, this is surprising. Figure 11.3 shows the areas in which acquirers in the AMR/ICME survey did not believe they were sufficiently detailed in their investigation.

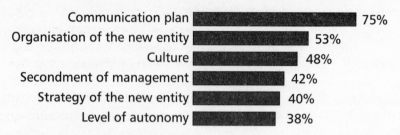

Subjects insufficiently considered before acquisition

Communication plan	75%
Organisation of the new entity	53%
Culture	48%
Secondment of management	42%
Strategy of the new entity	40%
Level of autonomy	38%

Figure 11.3 *Prepare a comprehensive integration plan (Source:* AMR/ICME survey).

The human resources issues which arise once a business has been acquired can be divided into three categories:

- human resource strategy
- communications
- cultural integration.

HUMAN RESOURCE STRATEGY

Acquirers who take human resource management seriously tend to incorporate human resource planning within their overall business planning process. Such companies tend to find it relatively simple to introduce their human resources strategy to new acquisitions. Difficulties do still emerge where the acquired company adheres to a mechanistic management model, where people issues are always subservient, for example, to commercial or engineering objectives.

The development and implementation of a human resource strategy can make the difference between success and failure. An important early step to take after acquisition is to audit the business in a way that would not have been possible earlier. This will provide detailed information on culture, organisation and management. Audit techniques such as attitude surveys, questionnaires, structured interviews and so on make it possible to anticipate how initiatives planned to influence or change one dimension will affect the others.

Case Study 8 illustrates the danger of failing to address man-

agement and cultural integration with a coherent human resource strategy.

CASE STUDY 8: TELFOS PLC: PREDATOR TURNS INTO PREY AS THE DIFFICULTY OF CULTURAL INTEGRATION IS SEVERELY UNDERESTIMATED

Telfos, a UK listed railway engine manufacturer, acquired one of
Central Europe's largest locomotive manufacturers, Ganz-Marvag
of Budapest, in 1988. The deal appeared to be a bargain with a little
over £2 million changing hands, and a further £9 million of consideration nominally paid in the form of intellectual property.
Approximately 1500 people were employed at Ganz-Marvag; no
one knew the exact number.

Although action was taken quickly, many of the first steps were
the wrong ones, as insufficient preparatory work had gone into
understanding how the business operated. The rapid series of decisions to hire, fire and reorganise proved counter-productive. Three
hundred Polish engineers were laid off. It turned out that they
included some of the company's best talent. The unrealistic expectations of the Hungarian workforce shocked the British management. Many workers believed that they would be in line for pay
increases as a result of the acquisition; it never occurred to them
that they might have to alter working practices. Equally, the incom-
ing management underestimated the lack of understanding by
workers of a need to change. To make matters worse, there was a
near-total absence of any quality standards or workable management systems. Again, there was little understanding of why standards and systems are essential.

An education programme communicating the values and benefits of Western-run businesses was put in place some nine months
after the acquisition. Although the message was reasonably well
understood in the first instance, it did not result in an instant change
in attitudes and working practices.

A range of new systems was also put in place, with well-struc-
tured attempts at clear communication about their value. Despite
these efforts the systems were not smoothly followed at first.

The whole process was managed by a highly capable managing
director who was a Hungarian-born, western-trained railway

equipment specialist. Other senior executives capable of understanding both cultures were also hired. However, despite these pragmatic management actions and the recruitment of the right managers the gap between the UK quoted company culture and that of a former command economy employer was always too wide to bridge.

Jenbacher Werke, the Austrian carriage manufacturer, watched the overstretched British group lurch from one disaster to another with a growing sense of opportunity. As Telfos shareholders became increasingly dismayed at the performance of the group, Jenbacher's takeover bid for Telfos came as a welcome relief to institutions which were fully prepared to sell out and cut their losses.

Communications

It is crucial that internal communications are effective from the moment the contract is signed. The way in which the news of the change in ownership is communicated to the management and staff of the target company must be meticulously planned. As soon as the deal is signed the plan must swing into action so that employees and other important stakeholders hear the news from the acquirer before they hear it on the radio, see it on television or read about it in their newspapers. Fuchs, the German oil group, made no satisfactory employee communication for six months after its successful hostile bid for Century Oils. Morale collapsed, employees left and the target's performance had still not met expectations five years after the acquisition.

The communications strategy should be designed around a careful consideration of three factors:

- the audiences who will receive the message, taking their style, expectations and fears into account
- the message to be delivered, promoting the core values of the acquiring company and the position of the acquired company under new ownership
- how the message will be delivered including the people and the media that will be used.

Responsibility for the communications programme cannot be

vested entirely in any one individual – management has a collective responsibility to communicate with the workforce – but it is sensible to give one of the new management team the specific role of co-ordinating the design and implementation of the communications process.

Cultural Integration

Integrating the culture of two individual businesses is seldom straightforward: even where there are obvious commercial synergies between them, the cultural fit is rarely perfect. In some acquisitions cultural integration is not considered relevant. This can be a mistake, handicapping later development; even when an acquired business genuinely does not need to be integrated, it is usually imperative that management systems are brought into line so that reporting procedures can operate effectively.

Figure 11.1 shows the correlation between the closeness of culture and the success of integration.

A well-designed culture survey will define the company's culture, its values, the prevailing behavioural norms, and the way management directs the business. The results will suggest ways to bring the two cultures together. One successful method can be to set up joint teams to work on projects across the business.

SECONDING MANAGEMENT

Sending in a management team can be an excellent way to overcome many of the human resource integration problems. Obviously the management team should be well chosen to reflect the requirements of the newly combined business. Figure 11.4, taken from the AMR/ICME survey, sets out the correlation between those acquisitions where a management team was sent in early on during integration and the achievement of the initial acquisition objectives and the quality of post-acquisition atmosphere.

This section of the guide has demonstrated the importance to acquirers of taking human resources seriously. As expertise is

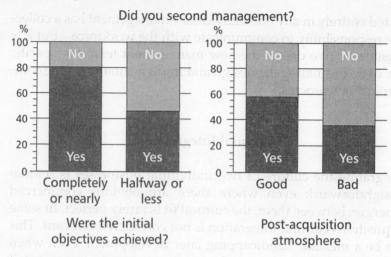

Figure 11.4   *Send in a management team* (*Source:* AMR/ICME survey).

not always available in-house, companies often turn to consultants for assistance.

Checklist 6 summarises the main issues to be considered for
human resources integration.

CHECKLIST 6

Human Resources Integration Checklist

Will your organisation and style suit the business and its markets?

Can management skills be properly assessed during due diligence?

How will the management style and culture in the target be assessed?

What sort of extra management resources will be needed after the acquisition? How soon will they be put in place?

Will a detailed integration plan be prepared before the change in ownership is announced?

Who will manage the integration process and who will be their backup?

How quickly will you be able to implement changes?

How will both sets of employees be informed about events during the integration process?

How will you decide which human resource management systems should be integrated and which left alone?

What will the policy be on transferring key managers between the organisations?

What are the contingency plans if the target's managers leave?

What will be the policy for compensating directors who are removed?

What exchange of specialist skills between the two businesses will be useful?

How will redundancies be handled?

Are the remuneration policies of the two businesses compatible and what will be the cost of aligning them if that is necessary?

How will successful integration be rewarded?

12
Joint Ventures and Strategic Alliances

THE LOGIC

The early 1990s saw a decline in the level of merger and acquisition activity, but an increase in the number of joint ventures and strategic alliances. Strategic alliances are distinct from mergers in that both sides retain their identity. They allow a business to achieve its product or market objectives at a lower cost than the alternatives of direct investment or acquisition. They are also distinct from trade investments, which often have the objective of allowing a potential acquirer to gain first-hand experience of the target.

Joint ventures and strategic alliances are formed for a variety of reasons. Some of the most appropriate ones are as follows:

- *To optimise distribution.* Guinness combined with LVMH, and Coors with S&N to expand their sales through established channels in unexploited territories. Guinness and LVMH subsequently expanded their alliance to 20 territories.
- *To achieve critical mass or economies of scale.* Independent retailers have formed buying clubs to combat the growing power of the multiples. Vineyard co-operatives reduce production costs and increase marketing power. French distributors of tableware for the hotel and catering sector have formed buying clubs to improve their purchasing power.
- *To overcome barriers to market entry.* Many joint ventures have

been created to enable companies to enter big emerging markets such as China, Poland and Brazil.

- *To overcome management or shareholder resistance to the outright sale of a business.*
- *To avoid a bid.* The alliance between Wessex Water and Waste Management largely protects Wessex against potential bidders, although the primary reason for it was to give Wessex access to a significant stream of non-regulated income, and to allow Waste Management into new geographical markets.
- *To consolidate resources and reduce competition in declining industries.* There are numerous examples in the defence industry, including the missiles businesses of Matra and BAe.
- *To spread development cost among a number of partners.* Airbus was formed because none of the European aircraft makers could compete alone with Boeing.
- *To manage risk.* These can be geographic or political risks. Companies may wish to keep exposure to certain countries or to a certain political situation to a minimum.
- *To combine separate skills in order to win a contract.* Britain's national lottery was won by a consortium involving De La Rue and Racal. Losing bids were also consortia.

Three questions to ask before establishing a strategic alliance or joint venture are:

- Do both parties bring a genuine skill or resource to the venture?
- Do both parties stand to gain?
- How will things be sorted if the venture goes wrong?

Japanese companies are notorious for their aggressive approach to joint ventures, and for only entering into one if they stand to learn more than their partners. Returning managers are required to debrief their colleagues fully on what they have learnt. This approach may well be valid in many cases. However, the human element, and the importance of building the relationship on trust, shared objectives and common rewards, means that it will not work in all cases.

Joint ventures should not be entered into lightly, as unravelling them can waste significant resources. However, unlike acquisitions, an exit route from the joint venture should always be considered in advance. This is often overlooked and can lead to difficulty in an area where there is little legislation. Discussing potential exits up front can help to highlight potential tensions. Otherwise the steps to take before establishing a joint venture are broadly similar to those that should be taken before making an acquisition.

REDUCING THE RISK

The following guidelines will enhance the chances of a joint venture's success:

- *Mutual need.* Each partner must take whatever steps are required to ensure that the other partner continues to benefit from the joint venture. This can be even more important than control.
- *Shared objectives.* Many companies are only familiar with relationships. Alliances require the parties to agree what needs to be achieved, and to collaborate on achieving it.
- *Shared risk.* All the risk cannot be loaded on to a single party. These risks can be both economic and personal.
- *Proven benefits.* The same procedures as for acquisitions should be used to prove that the venture will deliver the required returns.
- *Political support.* Each party should attempt to build up widespread political support internally in advance of the venture being established in order to create the best atmosphere for the new entity.
- *Relationships and trust.* The most successful joint ventures are based on trust that has been carefully and delicately built up by both sets of management. Contracts should be drawn up in such a way as to generate trust and enthusiasm as well as to minimise downside risks.
- *Autonomous management.* A joint venture should have its own board and a single reporting system. Its objectives should be defined clearly, and as simply as possible.
- *Disputes.* Potential disputes are obviously best ironed out at the start. However, an effective mechanism to solve disputes is

required, which could involve appealing to a higher management team.

- *Warning signs.* Attention should be paid to early signs of potential termination by the partner, such as inflexibility in adapting operating procedures, a combative negotiating style, conflict over management appointments and a reluctance to reinvest.
- *Exit strategy.* This should be agreed upfront. The most common exit route is that one of the partners takes control of the whole entity.

CONCLUSION

Although the sharply increased popularity of joint ventures and strategic alliances in the early 1990s was a response to the economic circumstances of the time, they should not be seen as a passing fad. In the right circumstances joint ventures can work; however, they are not always a long-term solution and they are not an outright alternative to acquisition.

Appropriately structured and well-managed joint ventures and alliances can allow both partners to achieve their objectives at a lower cost than most other development routes.

13
Acquiring in Europe

LESS OPPORTUNITY TO ACQUIRE

In continental Europe fewer businesses are bought and sold than in the UK and North America. As a rule of thumb, there are about half as many acquisitions in each of the main continental countries as there are in the UK. Some of Britain's most successful acquirers such as BTR and formerly Hanson have made few acquisitions in continental Europe. Reed International merged with Elsevier to tackle continental Europe.

In most continental European countries different rules apply to the way in which corporate control is managed and altered. In some cases, baffled Anglo-Saxons get the impression that there are no "normal" rules for corporate control. Continental companies use mergers and acquisitions as a vehicle for corporate growth far less frequently than their Anglo-Saxon counterparts.

Hostile takeover bids are discouraged and therefore fairly rare. When they do take place, they are often viewed as an outbreak of deviant behaviour, and as a practice best left in the Anglo-Saxon world. The long-running battle between Continental and Pirelli led to no outcome and left many observers bemused as to its logic, particularly as the hostile bid mechanism does not position the hostile bidder favourably from the outset. The Deutsche Post bid for Deutsche Postbank was particularly strange. The bidder and target shared the same parent, the German government, and the politically charged spat was born more out of rivalry between the chief executives than out of shareholder logic.

As well as there being less opportunity to acquire there is also less need to acquire in continental Europe. Average dividend rates are lower, meaning that profit retention levels are higher. This makes rapid organic growth easier to achieve using retained earnings and reduces the need for rights issues.

The justification for acquisitions in continental Europe can be very different. Acquirers sometimes base justification more on long-term strategic vision than on any quantifiable benefit to shareholders. The wholesale acquisition of companies in former Eastern Germany by West German business was seen more as a rescue effort (by West Germans, at least) rather than aggressive expansion policy. Table 13.1 later in this chapter sets out the varying reasons for acquisition for British, French and German companies.

An interesting example of comparative styles is that of Deutsche Bank's acquisition of Morgan Grenfell. The premium paid could only have been justified in terms of a long-term strategic perspective. Long-term thinking was also demonstrated when a rogue trader at Morgan Grenfell ran up substantial losses and the Germans rapidly stepped in with £180 million of rescue capital for one of its major European funds. All of this happened as the bank was committing itself to more Anglo-Saxon management techniques through the appointment of Rolf Bruer as chief executive.

On the Continent the approach to corporate finance is different. In the UK and the US the analysis of shareholder value, of acquisition possibilities, of the trade-offs between short-term financial and long-term strategic factors are all standard practice. They occupy much less management time in continental companies. The words "shareholder value" do not even exist in German – the English is used, underlining its foreign origin.

PERFORMANCE

Some bankers argue that European companies lag behind US and UK counterparts, delivering less to their shareholders, and that it is inevitable that this will change. Morgan Stanley calculates that US companies gave shareholders a much better return

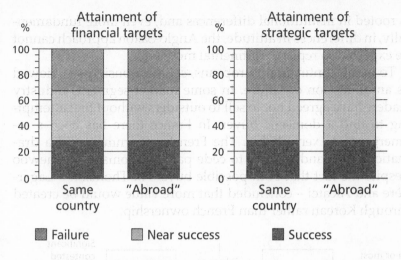

Figure 13.1 Cross-border success rates (*Source:* AMR/ICME survey).

on capital employed (20.4%) than European quoted companies (12.4%) in 1995.

There are some signs of change as Lyonnaise des Eaux and Commerzbank now publish return on capital employed targets, but there is a long way to go until European companies bow to the financial demands of shareholders in the same way as Anglo-Saxons. In defence of European performance, it should be noted that differing tax and accounting rules may make the gap appear wider than it really is.

Figure 13.1, taken from the AMR/ICME survey, shows that the performance of cross border acquisitions is less good than that of domestic deals. Interestingly, acquirers are much more tolerant of the performance of their cross border acquisitions in strategic terms than in financial terms.

THE CONTINENTAL DIFFERENCE

The differences between the two approaches to acquisition is the result of a long history of different approaches to corporate control. The single market and the globalisation of capital markets will inevitably have an impact. However, as the divergence is rooted in institutional differences and, even more fundamentally, in differences in attitude, the Anglo-Saxon approach cannot be expected to replace continental models.

To many continental Europeans, selling a business is viewed as an admission of failure. In some market segments industry leaders have agreed not to sell to outsiders without first attempting to find a domestic buyer. In France there has been a re-emergence of xenophobia. The French government did a dramatic U-turn and refused to cede part of Thomson to Daewoo despite the fact that both possible buyers of Thomson – Lagardère and Alcatel – concluded that more value would be created through Korean rather than French ownership.

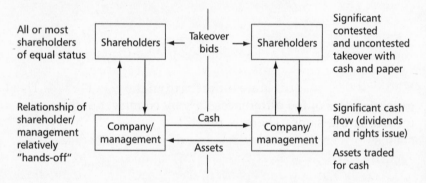

Figure 13.2   *Anglo-Saxon model for corporate control (Reproduced by permission of Finance Director International 1992).*

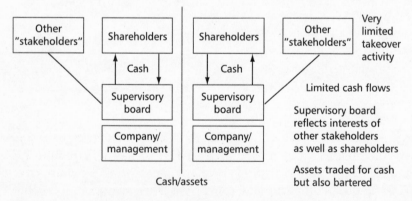

Figure 13.3   *Northern European model for corporate control (Reproduced by permission of Finance Director International 1992).*

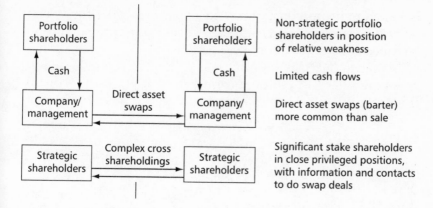

Figure 13.4 *Southern European model for corporate control (Reproduced by permission of Finance Director International 1992).*

Structural barriers to acquisitions are legion on the Continent, with patterns of ownership and the relationships between shareholders and managers quite different from those in the UK. The precise causes of the differences vary by country, but the consequence is the same. There is much less scope for the type of acquisition activity seen in the UK and US markets. Figures 13.2, 13.3 and 13.4 set out three comparative models.

There are three major differences between the Anglo-Saxon and continental ways of owning and funding businesses, which have implications for potential acquirers. The differences are:

- ownership
- quoted company conventions
- cross shareholdings.

Ownership

Much more industry is either state owned or privately owned in continental Europe; fewer firms conform to the UK and US model of the public limited company. In the UK there are over 2000 quoted companies, in Germany there are only 500. With fewer quoted companies there are fewer possible hostile acquisition targets. Also there are fewer opportunities to buy subsidiaries or divisions of quoted companies. Ownership of private companies is more likely to remain within the family, or succession is often organised far in advance of any change.

Quoted Company Conventions

The rules of conventions of corporate control within quoted companies are different and more constraining than in the Anglo-Saxon model, for very different reasons in different countries. In the Netherlands and Germany, two-tier boards effectively block changes in control by representing management's and workers' interests just as strongly as shareholders'. Indeed, in the Netherlands, the supervisory board is effectively a self-perpetuating oligarchy scarcely answerable at all to the nominal owners. In France, the top management of the Lagardère Group is all-but unimpeachable, despite owning only a tiny percentage of the overall business.

Cross Shareholdings

In Italy Mediobanca, Italy's leading merchant bank, exerts more control than ordinary shareholders through its network of alliances in the corporate sector.

Elsewhere, complicated webs of cross-shareholdings and different voting rights attached to different classes of share confuse lines of control. Messrs Berlusconi and de Benedetti's fight for control of the publisher Mondadori reached deadlock when Berlusconi had a majority of votes at ordinary shareholder meetings, while de Benedetti had the majority at extraordinary meetings. Neither could gain a mandate for change. Resolution came through a typically Italian asset swap. The conclusion is that the market for corporate control did not produce a clear winner, which would bother an Anglo-Saxon a lot more than an Italian. De Benedetti again used similar tactics to be re-elected to the board of Olivetti two weeks after resigning. He achieved this even though 70% of shares were held by international investors, who had to accept only a single non-executive director as protector of their interests.

A DIFFERENT ATTITUDE TO SHAREHOLDERS

These institutional barriers are backed by a fundamentally different way of thinking about corporate control. There is no single continental European way. The objectives, as well as the rules, of the market for corporate control diverge from Anglo-Saxon norms differently by region.

In northern Europe and Scandinavia, the objective of shareholder value itself is questioned, most notably in the Netherlands. Shareholders are perceived as just one among several stakeholders – alongside workers, managers, banks, founding families, consumers and society at large: non-financial objectives drive managers as forcefully as financial ones. Klaus Liesen, chairman of Rhurges and of the supervisory board of Volkswagen is publicly sceptical of the drive for shareholder value, arguing that the correct definition of shareholder value is the pursuit of long-term strategy.

In France, Spain, Italy and to a degree in Germany, family ownership and control are still common, so shareholders' interests do weigh heavily in the minds of directors since they are one and the same. In France and Italy there are notable quoted companies such as Matra Hachette, PSA and Fiat under family control. These family interests often have non-financial as well as wealth-maximising aspects.

The continuation of family involvement in management, the maintenance of brand names and product specifications developed over generations of family control, and the family firm's role in the local community can be as important to the private owner as making more money. These factors emerge frequently in discussions about possible acquisitions or alliances and they cannot be dismissed by Anglo-Saxons. The concept that there is a price for any asset which can be achieved in an efficient market, and that shareholders should seek to attain that price, is simply not as dominant in continental Europe as it is in the UK and the USA.

In France the network of management relationships extends on an informal basis through an alumni network. Graduates of ENA (Ecole Nationale d'Aministration) dominate senior management positions. The Lancer Boss example set out in Case Study 9 shows how in Germany the network operates through banks.

CASE STUDY 9: LANCER BOSS: CONFLICTING ATTITUDES TO CORPORATE CONTROL

In 1994, both the UK and the German parts of the Lancer Boss Group (the privately owned Bedfordshire based forklift truck producer) were badly hit by recession. Two banks – one in the UK the other in Germany – were funding the businesses to the tune of tens of millions of pounds. The group then ran into further difficulties with its German subsidiary Steinbock Boss GmbH, on which Lancer UK was dependent for around 40% of components. Jungheinrich, the large German lift-truck producer, sensed an opportunity and announced an interest in acquiring Steinbock Boss, the German end of the operation.

The German banks were keen to pursue a domestic solution for Steinbock's problems and strongly supported the deal. However, Steinbock's directors and Sir Neville Bowman-Shaw, Lancer Boss's British chairman, rejected the deal because it would have involved the break-up of the group.

In response the German banking group – led by Bayerische Hypo Bank – withdrew its support from Steinbock, which had been trading within its banking limits. Consequently the administrator – Werner Fogel, a German lawyer – was called in to Steinbock Boss on 8 April.

On the same day the UK operations were forced to follow the same route, due to the interdependence between the two group companies. The accountants Grant Thornton were named administrative receivers for Lancer Boss in the UK. Sir Neville Bowman-Shaw accused the German banking group of acting precipitately by withdrawing facilities from Steinbock Boss. Hypo Bank denied this charge on the basis that negotiations had been taking place for months.

Mr Griffiths of Grant Thornton contested that the group would be worth more if both parts were sold together, consequently he was keen to maintain the links between the UK and German operations. His problem, however, was that he was left in the unusual situation for a UK receiver of lacking full control of the company he was trying to sell. The power to sell Steinbock lay with the German administrator, who, along with the German banks which had appointed him had other ideas. They wanted Steinbock to be sold as quickly as possible to Jungheinrich, partly to reduce their own losses but also to ensure that Steinbock's future was clear before the Hanover Fair – Germany's leading exhibition of industrial equipment – later in April.

Before the acquisition of Steinbock by Jungheinrich in April 1994, other potential bidders had expressed considerable interest in the whole group as opposed to just Steinbock. However, Grant Thornton's hands were tied and once Jungheinrich had acquired Steinbock, the UK receiver had to secure the vital trading relationship between Lancer Boss and its former German unit. Then the sale of Lancer Boss could proceed more like a regular UK receivership. Of course, now that Jungheinrich owned Steinbock it was in a powerful position in comparison to other potential buyers, which would have to sort out a relationship with the German company, or risk losing 50% of its business.

Nonetheless, the fact that there were three bids in the final negotiations gave the British receivers the opportunity to push up the price Jungheinrich was prepared to pay.

On 5 May 1994 Jungheinrich announced that it had acquired from Grant Thornton the Lancer Boss Group and associated companies in Great Britain, Ireland and Austria.

The receiver emphasised the cultural difference: "My argument is not with Jungheinrich, but with the system that allowed this to happen," said Mr Griffiths. "You cannot sell a business with £70 million of turnover in three or four days."

Conclusions

- Banks play a major role in corporate control in Germany. Sir Neville Bowman-Shaw believed that he owned Steinbock Boss and therefore had control over his German subsidiary. But he had a rude awakening when he discovered that the German banks were controlling the show.
- Local financing can be a double-edged sword: it can reduce a company's financial risk better than financing in the UK, but in Germany, due to the country's different rules on corporate control, UK shareholders can lose influence or even control.

- The sale of a company in Germany is more likely to be conducted through local networking than an open market sale. The German receivers sold the business to their favourite party, a local player, avoiding a sale on the open market.

NATIONAL MANAGEMENT STYLES

Table 13.1, derived from the AMR/ICME survey, sets out the comparative management styles between French, German and British acquirers.

The Anglo-Saxon difference in clearly set out acquisitions are negotiated much faster and British acquirers were the only ones to cite diversification as a reason to acquire.

OBTAINING INFORMATION

Many prospective acquirers in Europe are baffled by the difficulty of obtaining any volume of useful information on continental companies. The Anglo-Saxon openness is not mirrored on the

Table 13.1   *National management styles.*

Nationality of acquirer	Negotiation period	Autonomy left to target	Strategic objectives	Main criteria to assess value
France	Over six months	High	International cover	Management skills Functional aspects (e.g. production)
Austria, Germany and Switzerland	Over six months	None	Critical mass	Geographical cover Market share Potential synergies Technology
United Kingdom	Under six months	Low	Diversification Penetration	Target's market and financial situation

continent. Only in France does a system equivalent to the UK's Companies House exist, which provides useful and detailed financial information on businesses. In Germany the equivalent structure is in place but over 95% of companies pay the minimal annual fine which allows them to avoid reporting. Shareholder details are public information in Germany, but they can be tortuous to obtain.

Of course, information is available. Some Europe-wide databases can provide useful guidelines, although their quality is varied and using a single information source across continental Europe is inevitably dangerous, since no one system has the best coverage of each market. Obtaining access to local networks, whether they are of advisers, suppliers or any other form of stakeholder is an excellent way to understand a target sector or company.

Similarly, the basic approach to commercial due diligence can be used at an earlier stage in an acquisition programme to investigate the appropriateness of forming a relationship with one or more target businesses. It can also provide some useful guidance about how the best form of approach to shareholders and other stakeholders can be made.

MARKET LIQUIDITY

The market for corporate control, which allocates productive assets and businesses to the management teams best able to manage them, is clearly less liquid on most of the continent, but it does exist. Assets are traded between companies and new managerial arrangements are made, but not primarily through the mechanism of takeovers. Instead the market works predominantly through collaboration, share swaps, asset swaps and joint ventures.

When Fiat concluded that its holding in Telettra represented a huge research and development burden in a business not essential to its portfolio, its reaction was not to sell out to the highest bidder, but instead to wait two years until an appropriate swap opportunity appeared with CGE. Fiat gained assets from CGE which complemented its car business portfolio. The deal also entailed a share swap.

Share swaps like those between Paribas and Banca Commerciale Italiana might appear meaningless to a UK company. For many continental companies they create relationships that later result in asset swap or joint venture opportunities. And joint ventures through cross-holdings such as Thyssen with ABB in railways, and Renault with Volvo in trucks and buses, are mechanisms to create coherent businesses without the break-up of existing portfolios, and without aggressive takeovers. Airbus Industrie brought together its partners through a GIE (Groupement d'Intérêt Économique), involving no transfer of assets. The structure is of a not-for-profit organisation at the core, although the various partners are able to make profits (or receive subsidiaries) on their parts of the activity. Only some ten years after its creation is the company being moved to a more traditional structure.

GEC is one British company that has been successful in following the continental model. In preference to outright acquisition it has forged links with major continental groups through joint ventures such as GEC Alsthom and Matra Marconi space division.

So the market does exist, but it works by different rules. Figures 13.2, 13.3 and 13.4 set out three alternative models for the market for corporate control.

In the UK and the US the relationship between shareholders and managers is rich in terms of flows of cash (dividends and rights issues) but it is quite hands-off and independent; corporate control is traded through inter-shareholder deals driven by price, albeit at the initiative of managers.

In most continental countries, the cash flows through the external shareholder markets are smaller, and intercompany barter is the more common way to trade assets. In some countries, chiefly in the north, external flows and involvement are limited by concerns for other stakeholders. In others (above all in Italy) there are close links between major strategic shareholders and management, with complex webs of cross-shareholdings that provide the information and relation ships to drive asset swaps, and only limited reference to the more distant public investors.

REPATRIATING PROFIT

These more limited cash flows mean that the various continental systems are less well designed to return profits to shareholders than the Anglo-Saxon model. If a British investor is seeking to obtain what might be considered to be normal return on investment, this should be considered in detail when the deal is structured. Tax considerations will be vital.

If the intention is to use part of the profits to service local debt, or to reinvest in the business, along the lines of the local model, the problem will be less acute. However, given the typical demands of Anglo-Saxon shareholders the question must be asked as to how long this strategy will last and as to what happens next.

SIGNS OF CHANGE

These differences in the operation of the markets for corporate control are not likely to disappear rapidly, but there are some signs of change. The globalisation of capital markets is forcing those companies that are seeking Anglo-Saxon equity or a US listing to operate more on Anglo-Saxon lines. Also, budget pressures in Italy and France are driving privatisations, and the French government has loosened the restrictions on foreign investment into partially privatised companies. Chargeurs, the French retail and textiles group is splitting in two to boost its stockmarket capitalisation; in Germany, Hoechst, the chemicals group is considering demerger for similar reasons. German banks have reduced their shareholdings, allowing more company shares to be traded on the stock market.

In Germany second-generation owners of family businesses are expected to be more willing to sell out than their parents; they may also be more inclined to drive a hard bargain. The Institution for Mittelstandsforschung expects 10% of Mittelstand companies to change owners between 1996 and 2000. This would represent an unprecedented level of takeover activity, driven by the impending retirement of many founders of business who set up after the Second World War.

Spanish and Italian private companies may feel the need to internationalise to stay competitive, and this may create takeover or stake-building opportunities. Shareholders are also flexing their muscles. In the Netherlands, a mere minority shareholder, Torstein Hagen, has dared to challenge the management of Nedlloyd's right to manage as it sees fit. TI's acquisition of the Swedish company Forsheda was challenged by minority shareholders in Denmark, as they believed the purchase price was insufficient.

But on balance it is unlikely that these forces will shift the rules of the game radically, or do more than marginally increase the liquidity of the markets.

There is no political will for change, and indeed no agreement that shareholders should have pre-eminent rights over other stakeholders: there is no intent, and no need, to reduce the proportions of German and Italian business which are privately rather than publicly held. There are no firm plans to standardise shareholder voting rights.

Above all, there are no mechanisms in place to harmonise the different attitudes and conventions which have developed in different countries. As a result, European harmonisation displays an intriguing asymmetry: product and labour markets are close to being fully free and increasingly harmonised; capital exchange controls have gone; a single currency may even be on the way; but the rules and objectives of the markets for corporate control differ widely and will probably continue to do so.

The asymmetry of the market harmonisation process poses a significant challenge to UK companies. While sales expansion into European markets, and the establishment of Europe-wide production facilities and of European brand names are all recognised challenges, one of the classic tools of expansion – acquisition – is either unavailable or often needs to be executed quite differently.

DOING BUSINESS ON CONTINENTAL TERMS

If British managers are to be successful in continental Europe they must master new skills and approaches. The Continent is not going to conform rapidly with the Anglo-Saxon model and the different attitudes to corporate control are part of the culture of each country. The British owner-managers of Lancer Boss discovered this to their cost when it emerged that German banks actually controlled the bulk of its manufacturing operations (Case Study 9 on pp. 132–3 sets out the details).

British companies have needed to learn some continental ways of doing business and to think carefully how to communicate to shareholders the rationale of those ways:

- Companies negotiating with privately owned firms will need to address a wide range of factors other than price. Deals may need to preserve family control; minority stakes that give access to brand names and co-operation may need to be considered; and constraints upon subsequent freedom of action, such as of employment location may need to be accepted.
- Attitudes to minority stakes and to share swaps may have to change; these stakes may be one of the mechanisms required to build relationships that generate subsequent opportunities for asset swaps and collaborative agreements. Joint ventures and collaborative market approaches will play a greater role. One example of a changed attitude is that of Reed International, now merged with Elsevier: the group is now prepared to take minority stakes, which were ruled out before the merger. Stakes may need to be viewed as options, which open the door to future possibilities. Like all options, they are risky and some may turn out to be worthless while others may become a very valuable part of a portfolio.
- It is essential to develop a different set of skills including understanding and patience. Potential acquirers need to understand what motivates different European counterparts to act as they do. Patience is required to cope with the often long gap between agreeing to collaborate with a European firm and seeing the delivery of substantial quantifiable benefits.

For many UK companies these are major challenges, requiring profound shifts of philosophy. Minority stakes have traditionally received a poor press in Britain: experiences such as Metal Box's with Carnaud, and Dunlop's with Pirelli, have helped reinforce a suspicion of involvement and responsibility without control. Many UK companies and banks cannot see any purpose behind the nominal shareholding swaps often made between major continental players.

On the positive side:

- GEC has been successful in creating European joint ventures
- Emap used joint venture and then acquisition to establish a strong presence in France
- Reed International has increased its share rating following the merger with Elsevier
- Redland dominates part of the German building materials industry.

An example not to follow, however, is that of exhibitions organiser Blenheim, which was at first spectacularly successful in acquiring private companies in Europe and which obtained a French listing in addition to its UK quotation. Its policy of over-paying, financial engineering and taking short-term pricing decisions did not reflect either shareholder or customer needs; the company fell dramatically from favour and was finally taken over by United News.

THE MANAGEMENT PROBLEM

There is no shortage of differences in attitudes to corporate control and shareholder value. The extent of these differences has been set out with reference to seeking to acquire. To an operational manager, this is only part of the problem. Once a business has been purchased, these cultural differences do not go away. In fact they can become more important and form the basis for fundamental disagreement over day-to-day management and strategy. Chapter 11 deals with these management issues in detail.

CONCLUSION

To be successful, UK companies need to operate effectively in continental Europe, so they need to develop these new styles of approach and to explain the value of European expansion to shareholders. This last challenge may well be the hardest one to face. The benefits of long-term collaborations, of minority stakes, of deals with private companies hedged round with restrictions, of options for the future, may not show up quickly in earnings, and may well be treated with suspicion by shareholders traditionally wary of fuzzy managerial objectives and ill-defined strategic visions. But in the longer term, failing to exploit the opportunities that Europe offers may be worse, even by the strict standards of shareholder value.

14
Timing

FEAST OR FAMINE

In the acquisition process there is invariably too little or too much time available for just about every task.

To make a succesful acquisition, the acquirer needs to have three key elements available, at the right time. These are:

- financial resources
- appropriate management resources and skills for integration
- an operating structure into which the new business can fit.

Getting this combination right is not easy, but it is largely within the potential acquirer's control. Frustratingly, if the potential acquirer's business does not have these critical elements in place, management has to accept that attractive opportunities must be passed over.

When the correct resources and skills are in place, a circumstance beyond the acquirer's control comes into play. The right acquisition candidates need to be available, at the right price.

FINDING THE OPPORTUNITIES AND AVAILABILITY

Patience is essential during any acquisition search. Although drawing up a shortlist of potential targets and conducting a preliminary evaluation of each one can be completed relatively quickly, the subsequent steps can be painfully slow.

When approaches are made to the owners of companies which are not for sale it takes a minimum of one year for a deal to be agreed, if there is one to be done at all. Although waiting for a change in ownership intention is frustrating, the potential acquirer who made the approach has the advantage that when the opportunity does arise there is an excellent chance that the fit will be appropriate. After all, it was the acquirer that selected the target. There is also a reasonable chance that this patient approach will be rewarded with exclusive negotiations.

When an acquirer is relying on a network of intermediaries to find companies for sale the process can be even slower. The number of opportunities thrown up may be greater than in a focused search, but their quality will be inferior. Numerous candidates will need to be reviewed and the vast majority will be rejected for reasons of fit. Any acquirer using this method of candidate identification must count on at least one year of searching before some appropriate opportunities have been identified.

Those acquirers which are prepared to be patient in their courtship of targets even find that turning down opportunities is not always the end of the story. In some cases a vendor will find no buyer at the price level sought. It will then return to its preferred buyer, even if it declined the opportunity. In other cases, prospective acquirers who lost on price find that the competitor that overpaid encountered difficulties and itself became available, or decided to reverse out of its position and sell some of its subsidiaries.

INVESTIGATION AND DUE DILIGENCE

It is very rare that there is sufficient time available to the acquirer and the advisers to conduct all of the investigations in the absolute detail required for a perfect understanding of the business. A number of factors can limit the time available. These include the announcement of the acquirer's or vendor's results; cycles in the seller's business such as annual contracts; competition among buyers or an aggressive intermediary running the timetable. In the case of very fast-growing businesses, there is some advantage to the buyer in concluding the transaction rapidly as valuation is based, in part at least, on forecasts of future performance. These will have been the subject of detailed negotiation and will inevitably differ after the negotiation period.

With so much time pressure and the onus on the acquirer to determine the value of the company for sale, the orchestration of the investigation and the due diligence process becomes critical. The potential acquirer should have a clear vision of which issues are important, how much attention should be paid to each one and who will be conducting the various parts of the investigation.

IMPACT ON THE COMPANY FOR SALE

Both sides have an interest in seeing a rapid conclusion as the value of almost any business will start to decline from the moment that it is put up for sale. The following factors can have a negative impact on value:

- Staff morale and motivation typically suffers as uncertainty about the future of the business emerges and concerns are raised over careers.
- Recruitment can become more difficult as senior candidates will be uncertain of the stability of the company, and of their proposed role.
- Staff may be inclined to make short-term decisions.
- Competitors will seek to exploit any rumours about a business being for sale by implying a possible lack of commitment and an uncertainty of supply.
- Customers may be wary of making firm long-term commitments if ownership is uncertain.
- Major suppliers may become concerned about receiving payment.

These factors encourage sellers to maintain confidentiality for as long as possible and to seek to sell the business rapidly. If a seller fails to find a buyer, it should eradicate uncertainty and clearly state that the company is no longer for sale, both within the company and to those outside the business who knew it to be for sale.

PREPARATION FOR INTEGRATION

One of the critical success factors for adding value through acquisition is to act quickly to integrate the new business. Preparation is therefore essential. This preparation must be conducted at a stage when there is very little time available. A detailed integration plan should be developed during the later phases of negotiation. Equally a communications plan must be developed so that managers and employees in the new business understand from the first moment of new ownership where they stand and what is expected of them. All of this has to be achieved within a very difficult time constraint.

WHEN TO ACQUIRE

Finally, it is worth considering when a business is worth acquiring in the context of the business cycle.

A business may have a special value to an acquirer only at a certain point in time. For example, Pearson paid a profit multiple of over 100 to acquire Software Tool Works as it was judged to offer an inroad to a new market. The business would have had very different values 12 months earlier or 12 months later. It is essential that the acquirer times the purchase at a point in the combined development cycle of the two businesses when there is sufficient opportunity to exploit the synergies and add value. For example, acquiring a typewriter manufacturer to consolidate a declining market may make textbook sense. But the acquirer must be confident that the amount paid to the seller is not as much as the profits to be reaped on all future sales of typewriters and ribbons (which is a finite sum).

The most common reason for overpaying is a misjudged business potential or cycle. Many entrepreneurs who sell their businesses admit that one of the reasons for sale was a fear that their business would suffer in changing competitive and market conditions. Standard evaluation techniques as set out in Chapter 6 and the use of thorough commercial due diligence as set out in Chapter 7 should be used rigorously to avoid the pitfall of overpaying.

CONCLUSION

For experienced acquirers who are used to the "stop-go" nature of acquisitions, these questions of timing may seem very obvious. For those who are relatively new to acquisition, timing issues can lead to frustration, or to failure.

15
Conclusion

Acquisition is highly risky. Shareholders of sellers typically receive a lump sum for a business as it stands, while buyers have to back their judgement of the business and its market, in the hope of improved profits in the future. Many acquisitions fail, bringing both financial and managerial burdens to the acquirer.

However, as exemplified by Hanson in the 1980s, when acquisitions work they are an excellent method of creating growth by unlocking value.

The main points that have been made in this guide are set out in Checklist 7 overleaf on pp. 150–1.

CHECKLIST 7: CHECKLIST FOR SUCCESSFUL ACQUISITION

Start with a realistic analysis of your own strategy.

Consider alternatives to acquisition.

Be clear about how the acquisition meets your strategic objectives.

Focus on how the two businesses will combine to increase value.

Develop clear acquisition criteria.

Avoid opportunistic acquisitions, except when they clearly fit a predetermined strategy.

Adopt a systematic approach to finding companies in target sectors.

Use external researchers with a clear brief where appropriate to identify targets.

Make sure that the approach is made to the right people on the right basis.

Evaluate acquisitions using standard investment appraisal methods.

Never be tempted to pay too much for an acquisition. Do not give the seller the benefit of the synergies.

Use a combination of valuation techniques.

Always be prepared to walk away if the deal is not right.

Balance the various methods of reducing risks to suit the circumstances of each deal.

Identify key managers within the acquisition target; determine whether they will stay and how they will be motivated.

Prior to acquisition, conduct detailed commercial due diligence. This is one of the most important risk reducers.

List all assumptions that have been made.

Ask the "sponsors" of the deal if they would put their own money into it.

Plan the integration in advance so that it is clear how potential synergies will be achieved.

Act fast when integrating to maximise value and reduce uncertainty.

Do not underestimate the effort and investment required for integration.

Conduct a post-acquisition review to see what could have been done better.

Index